Inside the Minds of Mass Murderers: Why They Kill

Inside the Minds of Mass Murderers: Why They Kill

KATHERINE RAMSLAND

Westport, Connecticut
London

Library of Congress Cataloging-in-Publication Data

Ramsland, Katherine M., 1953–
    Inside the minds of mass murderers : why they kill / Katherine Ramsland.
      p. cm.
    Includes bibliographical references and index.
    ISBN 0-275-98475-3 (alk. paper)
    1. Mass murderers—Case studies. 2. Mass murderers—Psychology. 3. Serial
murderers—Case studies. 4. Serial murderers—Psychology. 5. Risk assessment.
I. Title: Why they kill. II. Title.
HV6515.R253 2005
364.152′3—dc22   2004018113

British Library Cataloguing in Publication Data is available.

Library of Congress Catalog Card Number: 2004018113
ISBN: 0-275-98475-3

First published in 2005

Praeger Publishers, 88 Post Road West, Westport, CT 06881
An imprint of Greenwood Publishing Group, Inc.
www.praeger.com

Printed in the United States of America

The paper used in this book complies with the
Permanent Paper Standard issued by the National
Information Standards Organization (Z39.48-1984).

10 9 8 7 6 5 4 3 2 1

*For John Timpane, whose research assistance and enthusiasm
for my projects have helped me more than he knows*

And for Sande and Dana, "phenomenal women"

Contents

Introduction:
Mass Murder
and Its Classifications

FIRST MASSACRE

In 1873, 31-year-old Alfred Packer accompanied a group of prospectors from Utah into the San Juan Mountains in Colorado to seek wealth from mining. The party arrived in January 1874 at Chief Ouray's Ute camp in northwestern Colorado, where they were urged to remain until spring. At that time of year, the mountain passes were treacherous. Nevertheless, six of these men were impatient to get to the mines, so they set out on February 9, Packer among them, heading to the Los Piños Indian Agency on Cochetopa Creek near Saguache and Gunnison. The rest of the intrepid party included Shannon Wilson Bell, Israel Swan, James Humphrey, Frank "Reddy" Miller, and George "California" Noon, who was only 18. Aside from Packer, that was the last time anyone saw these men alive.

The Colorado state archives contain photographs, artifacts, writings, and legal proceedings from the case. James E. Starrs, professor of law and forensic science at George Washington University, has documented it all in his newsletter, *Scientific Sleuthing Review*.

Over two months passed and people at the Indian agency wondered where the prospectors were. On April 16, Packer apparently arrived alone. He had wads of money, and though he said he had not eaten in some time, he asked only for whiskey. Since he'd hurt his leg, he said, and had fallen behind, he did not know where the others were.

His listeners suspected he was lying, especially after a guide walking the trail found strips of human flesh. From all appearances, Packer had killed the other prospectors, survived off their remains, and enriched himself with their assets. People began to demand the truth.

Eventually Packer admitted that the others had died of starvation en route or were killed in self-defense from one another's hunger-maddened attacks. Israel Swan, 65, had died first, and the others had eaten pieces of him. Then four or five days later, James Humphrey died and was also eaten. The third man to succumb—Packer referred to him in his initial confession as "the Butcher"—was Frank Miller, in an "accident" that occurred while Packer was searching for wood. The other two had decided to eat him, and Packer had returned to find this "feast" already in progress. Next to die was George Noon, who was shot by Bell. Then Bell had tried to kill Packer, according to Packer's own initial report, striking at him with a rifle, so Packer had killed him first. And that left only one.

A search party went out, led by Packer, who took them to the area where he believed he had last seen the others, but they failed to find the missing prospectors. He was arrested and jailed on suspicion of murder. People continued to search, but it was not until August that John A. Randolph, an artist sent out to Colorado for *Harper's Weekly* magazine, came into Slumgullion Pass and discovered five sets of human remains in a cluster near the Gunnison River. One set was missing a head and two appeared to be missing pieces of flesh. He realized that this had to be the lost party of prospectors.

Among the mostly skeletonized remains were pieces of torn clothing, blankets, and some flesh still on the bones, but because weather and animals had done some damage to the remains it was difficult to determine what had happened to the men. Their feet were still bound in the blankets, which they appeared to have torn to pieces for that purpose, and no shoes, cooking utensils, or guns were found around them.

The Hinsdale County coroner, W. F. Ryan, hurried to the spot with twenty other men to hold an inquest. A member of the original party from Utah, Preston Nutter, identified the remains as those of his former companions. Clearly they had not died one by one along the trail. All had died or been killed at that spot. The bodies were buried together in graves on a high bluff nearby, which became known as "Dead Man's Gulch."

A trial was planned, but Packer escaped. Years later he was brought back, tried, and found guilty, but then a legal oversight gave him a new trial. The legal proceedings indicate that he placed the blame on Shannon Bell, saying that Bell had killed the others and had tried to kill him, so he had struck out in self-defense. At no time did he say he had killed as a result of the extreme circumstance of starvation.

For over a century, people were divided on the issue of Packer's guilt or innocence, with many in Colorado declaring him a state hero. However, an exhumation of the remains of the violated prospectors in 1989, directed by Professor Starrs, provided evidence that suggested that several had been murdered. There were cuts on the arms and hand bones that were indicative of defensive wounds, as well as nicks that supported the possibility that they had been defleshed. While not everyone has agreed on how to interpret these signs, Starrs went on record in his newsletter as saying that Packer was a murdering cannibal and a liar.

If that is the case, then aside from atrocities committed during wars, family massacres, train explosions, settling the West, and the plunder of Native Americans, Packer may be the first official American mass murderer.

In personality and motive, Packer is rare. He did not develop fantasies of revenge, was not frustrated at work, did not kill to erase a family and start a new life, and was not part of a larger scheme to wipe out large numbers of people for some religious or political ideal. He may well have killed for mere self-enrichment. And he's not alone in this. While Packer may not have inspired criminologists to look into the phenomenon of mass slaughter—indeed, he is not mentioned in many textbooks—his case cannot be ignored in a psychological study that seeks to understand a mass murderer's mind. He appears to be among those for whom death was an accompaniment to greed. And that has been one of the many motives for massacre.

DEFINITIONS

There is some disagreement among criminologists on the definition of a "mass murder"—some use the term to cover all multicides, such as serial killings and any other occasion in which someone kills more than a single person. Some sources indicate that there must be at least three victims to classify an incident as a mass murder, a few set the number at three plus at least two wounded, and others settle on a minimum of four victims. Michael Kelleher in *Flash Point* adds yet another dimension when he provides examples of would-be mass murderers who went hunting for large numbers but managed to kill only one or two. By intent, this person would still be a mass murderer, perhaps more so than someone who had only three killings in mind from the start. Depending on the definition used, the numbers of mass murderers documented in authoritative studies will vary greatly.

Sometimes the nature of mass murder is defined according to the extent of fear produced in a community, sometimes by the killer's motive, by evidence of general emotional discord within the killer, or by how contained a series of killing events is—with the proviso that the more prolonged they are in terms of time and locations, the more likely it is that they would be considered under another category, spree killings. Mass murder can be carried out with firearms, bombs, poison, stabbing, or even choking (rare but possible, if the victims are all subdued, especially in sexual homicides). A mass murderer, according to the FBI's *Crime Classification Manual*, is someone who kills four or more people in close succession in a single locale, or in closely related locales (although just how close this may be is not specified). Spree killers, who may have motives, spontaneity, and ambitions similar to those of mass murderers, tend to travel over a series of loosely related or unrelated locations.

What we have learned about mass murderers over the past half century is that they are typically quite ordinary. They're reclusive, have few if any friends, and prior to the violent incident often have no criminal record. However, they do not easily absorb life's unfairness, and may have suffered a serious disappointment early in life, from which they received a psychic wound that may have impaired their ability to take things in stride. They tend to build up anger and let frustration fester, with minor incidents being perceived as major offenses, and impersonal ones as personal. Some stressor, such as a broken relationship, a grievous loss, or unemployment, may become a trigger that sets everything in motion, but it's more the straw that breaks the camel's back than a significant cause in itself.

The time period for mass murder can be minutes or hours—even days, with some religious homicides. Disgruntled killers often blame others for their failures and their motive is generally to strike back, to punish, to annihilate, and to exact as much damage as they can manage. Some want to make a statement, others do it for self-glorification, and still others just act out. The higher the death toll, some killers believe, the better they have succeeded at their ultimate goals. Their choice of targets may be irrational, and often does not even include the one against whom they wanted vengeance. Yet others are careful to kill only those on their list, so to speak. Some show signs of psychosis, but most have been judged sane at the time of the incident—even the psychotic ones.

Yet even with the attempts to simplify a definition, there may always be problematic cases. Marc Lépine, for example, blamed women for his life failures. As documented in the Montreal newspaper *The Gazette* on December 6, 1989, he armed himself and committed the worst multicide to that point in Canadian history. He went to the engineering school at the University of Montreal, separated the women from the men in one classroom, and started shooting. Six women died and three were wounded, but he didn't stop there. If he had, his case would be simple to categorize. Instead, he roamed the building, upstairs and down, shooting at whomever he found. Finally he entered another classroom, killed more students, and then turned his pistol on himself. While this may seem to some to be an example of "loosely related locales," consider the next two cases, which involve even more time and territory.

In August 1987, Michael Ryan, 27, a gun-loving, hypersensitive man, took an AK-47 assault rifle and several other weapons on a shooting spree in Hungerford, England, killing fifteen and wounding as many before retreating to his former school and turning the gun on himself. In Britain's *Daily Telegraph*, his rampage was clearly recorded. He began in the woods, killing a woman, and then drove home to shoot the family dogs. When his car failed to start, he set fire to his house and strode around town, covering two miles while shooting at random both acquaintances and strangers.

Then there is Martin Bryant, as documented by Margaret Scott in *Port Arthur: A Story of Strength and Courage*. On April 28, 1996, in Australia, he killed the two owners of Seaside Cottages, then took two semi-automatic rifles to a tourist area in Port Arthur, where in fifteen seconds he shot and killed twenty people. He also wounded fifteen. He then walked around shooting more, got into his car to drive a few hundred yards, killed more people, stole a car, killed again, took a hostage, and went back to the cottages, where he killed several people who were driving by. He also killed the hostage. His total in less than a day was thirty-five dead, eighteen wounded. He moved around quite a bit and killed people in several different areas, but not in the manner of classic spree killers, who generally stretch things out over days or weeks, or from one town or state to another.

And what about John Williams, arrested for the Ratcliffe Highway murders in London, England, in 1836? On December 7, he allegedly bludgeoned to death four people in one home, and twelve days later killed three more people at an inn. He killed himself before getting to trial, but assuming he was guilty, would Williams be considered an extended mass murderer or a serial killer?

In other words, while experts struggle to fit people into recognizable categories for easier analysis, people just do what they do, perhaps defying easy classification. Thus, while studying trends and general profiles has its value, so does a more detailed look at individual cases that takes into account the many variations.

For the purpose of this study, I tend to focus primarily on those who have killed at least four victims, but I sometimes make exceptions when it is clear that the killer's intent had been to annihilate far more but he (or she) had just been a lousy shot or had been thwarted in some manner.

OBJECTIVE OF THIS BOOK

Since the 1960s, incidents of mass murder have been on the rise. In *Flash Point*, Kelleher states that from 1976 until 1991, there were 350 separate incidents, claiming some two thousand victims. He goes on to note that since 1991, the incidence of mass murder has increased, as have the number of victims per incident, and the crimes have become more gruesome. He says that there have been approximately two to three mass murders each month, claiming up to two hundred lives per year.[1] Criminologists such as Jack Levin and James Fox attribute this to the easy accessibility of lethal weapons. It could also be influenced by greater social breakdown and by media emphasis on violence. Like serial killers, mass killers get headlines, and for those trying to make a statement, that exposure on television can be appealing, even if they intend to kill themselves in the process. It still may play a part in their rehearsal fantasies.

There are several resources available for learning about all the different mass murders that have occurred in the United States. It is not my intention to cover that same material, nor to offer an encyclopedic listing, although there will be overlap. While some books are offered primarily for criminological purposes, depicting categories, statistics, charts, and trends, this book is focused on the psychological factors involved in the development of a mass murderer. Of necessity, since the circumstances for mass murder can be quite varied, there is a tendency to categorize killers, such as "kids who commit mass murder at school" or "people who kill their families." Yet there are aberrant cases as well that do not fit into any particular category, and these should not be ignored as peripheral. I want to avoid stereotypes that hinder true comprehension.

On the news or in documentaries, for example, one might hear experts make blanket statements such as, "They're white males in their thirties or forties with military background who feel frustrated by circumstances." While that may be true of many types of mass killers, there are many exceptions—enough to make a psychological study of the subject worthwhile.

This is a psychological survey of mass murderers from around the world, with the heaviest concentration on those in America, that will illustrate a range of methods and motives of the phenomenon. It is also an effort to understand how threat assessment and risk management may be able to assist people in seeing the red flags early in those people about whom we might say, "I never saw it coming."

I have not tried to give a rendering to all known incidents. Instead, I have selected those that exemplify certain types of massacres or for which psychological data were available via trial reports or other sources. There are far more cases than I include in these pages, but often they repeat in pattern or motive those I have chosen. In essence, anyone can learn something from this study, whether they are seeking to identify mass killers who may be developing in their midst or making the study of such murderers into a career. Looking at the incidents in detail, and sometimes in a historical context, provides a sense of the many different types of mass murder, as well as a way to use these data for future threat assessment.

CHAPTER 1

Howard Unruh: America's First Modern Mass Killer

EARLY INKLINGS

It is commonly assumed that a man named Howard Unruh from Camden, New Jersey, was the first modern American mass killer. Yet prior to his murders, there were several incidents that indicate otherwise. Whether or not one includes the Alfred Packer expedition as a mass murder, there was another incident during the nineteenth century that qualifies.

In Campbell, California, in 1896, James Dunham showed some rather strange behavior. He had married a woman named Hattie Wells, according to the *San Jose Mercury* archives, who was from a wealthy family in Campbell. Shortly after she gave birth to their son, Dunham asked an attorney a seemingly ordinary question that sounded quite different in retrospect. He wanted to know whether the child of a man who had married into a well-to-do family would inherit everything if the members of the family all died. He apparently received the response he wanted, because one night in May he used an axe and a revolver to slaughter his wife, her mother, brother, stepfather, the family maid, and the farmhand. Afterward, Dunham escaped, and his 3-week-old son became the official heir to the entire estate. Dunham was never prosecuted for the six murders. Nevertheless, the community would not soon forget the events of that inexplicably brutal night.

Then in 1910, trade union confrontations led to the bombing of the *Los Angeles Times* newspaper offices, in which twenty people died and another twenty were injured. Two brothers, James and John McNamara, pleaded guilty and were sent to prison.

Less than two decades later, in 1927, another massacre made head-lines. School killings got the nation's attention during the 1990s, but few people realize that one of the deadliest actually occurred several decades earlier in Bath, Michigan, as documented in Grant Parker's book *May-day*. It all started with an angry man, Andrew Kehoe, 55, who initiated his actions by killing his wife. But his real target was the town itself and those who governed it. Meticulous and reclusive, he lived on a 185-acre farm and was reported to be cruel to his animals. Indeed, before he went on his murderous rampage, he bound his horses with wire and set the barn on fire. Perhaps what precipitated his rampage were his wife's chronic illness and the threat of losing the farm. The more money he lost, the more he blamed the town's ravenous need to raise revenue for services. The Bath Consolidated School, in particular, seemed bent on draining him, like some vampire. He'd resisted its development, but it was built anyway.

Though he detested the place, Kehoe agreed to work there as a main-tenance man. That gave him easy access, which he quickly exploited. Over a period of months, he purchased an explosive called Pyrotol, a World War I surplus product, and also bought dynamite. Inside the school, he worked day after day wiring charges together and envision-ing dead children. He managed to plant over one thousand pounds of explosives. At the same time, he wired his own home to explode with firebombs. On May 17, the day he bludgeoned his wife to death, he added items that could serve as shrapnel. He also cut down all of his fruit and maple trees, leaving them to stand on their stumps as if still intact. But his plan went beyond his own homestead.

The next day, as the children arrived for school, Kehoe detonated the bombs at his home. As townspeople rushed over to help, they heard an-other explosion in the distance: the school. Kehoe had abandoned his burning property and driven there in a truck full of dynamite for one more mission. Right after he set off that explosion, he beckoned the superin-tendent of schools, Emory Huyck, to his truck and then shot his rifle into the explosives in the back seat, detonating them. Huyck was killed, along with another man, as shrapnel flew through the air. Kehoe died, too, sliced into pieces and thrown into the garden of a nearby resident.

In the end, Kehoe largely failed, because a short circuit had prevented his handiwork from bringing down the whole school. Yet thirty-eight chil-dren and eight adults, including Kehoe, had died. Sixty-one others had been seriously injured.

Kehoe had left behind a sign, posted on his property, to explain his madness: Carefully hand-lettered on a piece of wood were the words,

"Criminals are made, not born." His remains were gathered and he was buried alone in an unmarked grave.

Less than two years later, and just one state over, another massacre made headlines; in *The Century of the Detective*, Jürgen Thorwald offers a detailed description in his analysis of the development of ballistics. It was February 14, 1929. Seven men waited that snow-blown morning around 10:30 A.M. in a red brick warehouse for the S-M-C Cartage Company on Chicago's North Side, at 2122 North Clark Street. Suddenly three men in police uniforms and two civilians arrived in a police car and went inside. Witnesses in the neighborhood heard the sudden explosion of machine guns. Then the police officers left the building and a dog inside began to howl. Neighbors found a bloody scene: the seven unarmed men lay on the floor, all having been shot in the back multiple times. The wall against which they had been lined up for the assassination was a gory mess of blood and tissue.

The victims were associates of mobster George "Bugs" Moran. He pointed the finger at Al Capone, while Capone, in Florida at the time, accused Moran. However, many people thought that the police had killed a gang in cold blood, so it was left to a ballistics investigation to unearth the true story. The shooters had left behind seventy cartridge casings and the weapons were identified as .45-caliber Thomson submachine guns.

Calvin Goddard, an early ballistics expert, arrived from New York as an independent investigator and fired each of the eight machine guns owned by the Chicago police. He then compared the results to evidence collected at the scene. No casings matched, which cleared the police. This meant that someone had impersonated police officers to commit the murders.

Ten months later, the police raided the home of one of Al Capone's hit men. They found two machine guns, which they gave to Goddard. He test-fired them and proved they were the weapons used in the massacre. This sent at least one of the killers to prison. The infamous St. Valentine's Day Massacre turned out to have been part of a gang war between Capone and Moran. Evidently the men had been lured there— and Moran was supposed to have been among them—by a call from Detroit indicating that a truck full of hijacked whiskey was coming in. Moran himself was late, and he just missed being victim number eight.

Although this bloodbath was a "hit" and was performed by a group, the massacre in Bath does indicate that social pressures mixed with mental illness had a toehold in America before Howard Unruh, and others like him, arrived on the scene. In 1934, Leo Hall murdered six people in a home that he had set out to rob; in 1942 and 1944, respectively, a lustful grocery clerk, James Simececk, killed a family of four, and a disgruntled man, Robert Dale Segee, set fire to a circus tent, killing 169. It took six years to pin the circus arson on Segee, after which he admitted to more arsons as well as the murders of five more people. However, Unruh was the first mass killer whom a team of psychiatrists had the opportunity to actually study for some indication of motive.

ACTING OUT

The prototypical mass murderer, the one who springs to mind when people use the term, cannot accept failure or an insult, real or imagined. He will harbor a grudge and he often feels that he must make a stand or get revenge on those who have brought him to a place he does not want to be.

In 1948, in Chester, Pennsylvania, 30-year-old Melvin Collins leaned out the window of the boardinghouse where he was staying and opened fire with a rifle. The *Philadelphia Inquirer* states that he managed to kill eight people and wound four before killing himself. His motives remained a mystery, but were somewhat clarified the following year when Howard Unruh did something similar not far away.

Unruh, whose name in German means "unrest," was a man who let his grievances simmer. He lived with his mother in her apartment in Camden, New Jersey, and much of his time had been spent thinking about those people who he believed had wronged him. He'd even made a list and had formed ideas about what he would do when the time was right.

Recently he had built a gate in the yard because his neighbors, who complained about his music, had asked him to stop using theirs when he went out. Even the act of building it had irritated him. He had gone off to Philadelphia that evening, across the Delaware River, to see a double feature. Reporters for the *Philadelphia Inquirer* later learned that he watched both movies three times through, but it's just as likely that he sat in the theater all that time steaming over his situation. Finally, around 3:00 A.M., he went home. That's when he saw that someone had stolen the new gate, and he believed he knew who. In his mind, the people in the neighborhood had ganged up on him and had been talking about him behind his back. He needed to teach them all a lesson. His "preconceived plan" would commence in the morning, on September 6, 1949.

Dressing in a brown tropical-worsted suit, white shirt, and striped bowtie, the slender, 6-foot recluse picked up his 9-mm German Luger and went out around 9:20 A.M. His mother had just left, frightened away by his demeanor, so she was out of the way. He could have taken his hunting knife, machete, or any number of guns from his impressive and lethal collection, but he favored the Luger. Unruh also grabbed a 6-inch knife and a tear-gas pen with six shells. Vaulting over a fence, he cut through several back streets before stepping out into the road.

The Cramer Hill area of Camden in 1949 was generally quiet, but that day, for a mere twelve minutes, the shooter disturbed the peace. As a predator circling his prey, using what he had learned about hunting enemies during his military stint in World War II, he approached his targets.

At the corner of Harrison and 32nd Street sat a bread delivery truck. Two kids were playing nearby. Unruh spotted the driver inside the truck. It was time. Shoving the Luger through the door, he pulled the trigger. But he missed. The man had ducked away.

"He missed me by inches," the unidentified driver later told the *Philadelphia Inquirer*. "I was seated in my bread truck going over my records and he walked up and shoved a pistol through the door at me. I thought it was a holdup. I tumbled into the back of my truck among the breadboxes. He fired one shot and, thank God, it missed me."[1]

The shooter walked along the street, back toward his home, but he planned to make several stops. Entering a shoe repair shop, he aimed the gun at John Pilarchik, 27, walked within a yard of him, and fired twice, taking his prey by surprise. He now had his first kill of the day. Unlike the bread man, the shoemaker had been on his list.

Various newspapers covered these events in retrospect, reconstructing the murders. The *Philadelphia Inquirer* offered extensive accounts, with maps and photos, as did the Camden *Courier-Post*. Later, a *New York Times* journalist, Meyer Berger, would win a Pulitzer Prize for his coverage.

Next door to the shoe repair shop was Clark Hoover's barbershop. When Unruh entered, Hoover, 33, was busy with a young client, a 6-year-old boy who sat on a white carousel horse. His mother, Catherine Smith, sat watching. It was a sweet scene, like something one might see in Norman Rockwell paintings, but it was about to become something more akin to a macabre masterpiece by Edvard Munch. Unruh took aim. The barber attempted to shield the boy, but he was too slow. The first bullet hit the boy in the head and the second one killed Hoover. Both dropped instantly to the floor. The shooter left as the boy's mother grabbed her son and went screaming into the street.

He headed for his next stop. Only moments had passed, but three people were dead. Passing a group of kids who raced for cover, Unruh lifted his weapon to shoot at a boy watching him from a window, but he missed. He attempted to enter a tavern but found it locked against him, so he shot two bullets into the door. The tavern's owner, Frank Engel, rushed up the steps to retrieve his .38-caliber pistol to be ready in case the madman broke in. But Unruh was otherwise occupied. Taking a moment to reload, he changed his strategy. It was time to find his true enemies, the Cohens, the neighbors who had persecuted him over the past two years and had asked him not to use their gate. They were at the top of his "List of Grudges."

Unruh was close to their drugstore. As he was about to enter, an insurance agent named James Hutton came out. He greeted Unruh in a friendly manner, but Unruh is said to have warned him with, "Excuse me, sir." Hutton did not move, so he received his own fatal bullet.

Now in the pharmacy, Unruh cornered his most important prey. He spotted Maurice Cohen and his wife, Rose, running up the steps to their apartment. Following them, he saw Rose go into a bedroom closet. Standing outside it, he fired three times through the door. Then he opened it and shot her in the head. Walking through the apartment, he encountered Maurice's elderly mother, 63, on the telephone. He killed her and then saw Maurice jump out a window onto a porch roof, so he followed.

The shooter hit Maurice with a bullet, sending him off the roof to the sidewalk below. Maurice had no time to recover, because Unruh had jumped down the steps and come out to the street, where he discharged another shot. Maurice died right there on the street, but he had succeeded in saving his 12-year-old son, who had hidden in a closet upstairs. Unruh reloaded again. Although he had eliminated his enemy, he was not yet finished.

Nearby, Mrs. Harrie and her 16-year-old son, Armond, were hanging clothing on a clothesline. Mrs. Harrie went into her house, followed by Unruh. According to her son, who ran into the house after Unruh, the killer shot at them five times. Unruh tried smacking Armond with the butt of the empty pistol, but before anyone could stop him, Unruh left. He now had shot nine people, killing seven.

Circling back, Unruh walked alongside the pharmacy and encountered a man in a car, Alvin Day, who had slowed down near the body of James Hutton, the insurance agent. Unruh leaned into Day's car and killed him. Then he walked over to a car stopped at a light and shot through the windshield, killing the female driver and her mother and wounding a 12-year-old boy in the back seat with a bullet through his neck. Next was the car behind this one, where he shot and wounded a young male, Charlie Peterson. He aimed his Luger at several other cars as well and shot into them.

Finally, he went into the tailor's shop: Zegrino, too, was on his list. By that time, a man who had been in line behind the cars into which the maniac had shot had driven to the nearest fire station, on 27th Street, six blocks away, to raise an alarm. The police were getting ready to rush to the scene.

When the tailor's wife, Helga, who had been married to Zegrino for only three weeks, saw Unruh enter, she got on her knees and, according to witnesses, begged, "Oh, my God, don't!" Without mercy, Unruh pointed his gun and shot her.

There would be one more. A 2-year-old boy, Tommy Hamilton, happened to look out his front window, so the shooter aimed and fired right through the glass, killing him.

Unruh attempted once more to get into a restaurant that stood at the end of River Road near Bergen Street, but failed; so as sirens wailed from a distance, he went around to the back and finally went home to his second-floor apartment. He'd been out for less than a quarter of an hour, but was running low on ammunition. "I ran out of bullets," he later said, "so I went home."[2]

In his wake, twelve people were dead—five men, five women, and two young children—and four were badly wounded—a man, a woman, and two teenagers. One of these would later die, bringing the death toll to thirteen. Had Unruh hit and killed everyone at whom he took a shot, the number of deaths would have been twenty-six.

The police were scrambling to go after Unruh, but he reached his apartment first and barricaded the door. People had now identified by name the rampaging shooter to the first arriving officers as a 28-year-old "religious nut," and all available police reserves were called in to surround his building. None had ever dealt with such an incident before.

Between fifty and sixty police officers surrounded the two-story gray stucco building that housed Unruh's apartment at 3202 River Road, behind and next to the Cohens' pharmacy and residence. Unruh was inside, and he shot from a window. The police had armed themselves with rifles and machine guns. For a time, the road was a site of confusion, with people in the milling crowd getting into the line of fire. No one quite knew what protocol they should follow. This kind of incident was almost unknown.

The officers shot into the apartment in what reporters called a "rain of gunfire" intended to drive the shooter out or kill him. Pedestrians formed a ring around the area and within half an hour, over a thousand people were watching. Several marksmen mounted themselves on the roof of a shed to get a clear shot into the room from which the suspect himself was steadily shooting.

Around this time, Freda Unruh, the shooter's mother, had started walking home. When she saw the police barricade and heard spectators shouting, she knew it was about her son, and she left the scene. She finally made her way to the home of her sister, five blocks away, who found a doctor to treat her. It was the sister's opinion that this had all been caused by "terrible experiences" that Howard had suffered during his military enlistment.

Philip W. Buxton, an assistant city editor of the *Camden Evening Courier*, looked up Unruh's phone number and called the home. To his surprise, a man answered, and the dialogue was reported in several area newspapers as the following:

"Is this Howard Unruh?" Buxton asked.

"Yes, this is Howard. What's the last name of the party you want?"

"Unruh," the editor told him.

"Who are you?" Unruh demanded to know. "What do you want?"

Buxton could hear the loud noise of bullets coming through the window, breaking glass. He identified himself as a friend and then asked, "What are they doing to you?"

"They haven't done anything to me yet," said Unruh, "but I'm doing plenty to them."

"How many have you killed?"

"I don't know yet—I haven't counted them. But it looks like a pretty good score."

The editor then wanted to know why he was killing people.

"I don't know. I can't answer that yet. I'm too busy. I'll have to talk to you later. A couple of friends are coming to get me." He slammed down the phone.[3]

Outside, the detectives on the roof moved close enough to lob a canister of tear gas through the broken bedroom window, which alerted Unruh, so he left that window and went into another room. When the canister proved to be a dud, he returned. As he came in, the detectives tossed in a second canister and the place slowly filled with stinging gas. It took another five minutes, but finally Unruh moved aside the white curtain upstairs, looked out, and said, "Okay, I give up. I'm coming down."

"Where's the gun?" a sergeant yelled up at him.

"It's on my desk, up here in the room. I'm coming down."[4]

He came out the door, unarmed, with three dozen guns trained on him, and surrendered. Forty-five minutes after he had taken his first shot,

Unruh was ushered through the angry crowd into a police car and driven away.

One observer murmured, "You gotta watch them quiet ones."

The police still did not understand what had happened. "What's the matter with you?" one officer asked Unruh. "Are you a psycho?"

"I'm no psycho," Unruh insisted. "I have a good mind."[5]

Not everyone was to agree.

ANALYSIS

At City Hall, detectives questioned Unruh for hours. At all times he seemed calm, as Meyer Berger reported for the *New York Times:* "Only occasionally excessive brightness of his dark eyes indicated that he was anything other than normal."[6]

To Camden County prosecutor Mitchell Cohen, Unruh admitted that before going to sleep the previous night he had made up his mind to go on this rampage. It had been premeditated and he willingly offered a detailed account, which was reproduced in several newspapers. "I shot them in the chest first," he explained, "and then I aimed for the head." Although some of the victims were preplanned targets, a few were shot just because they got in the way. "When I came home last night and found my gate had been taken," Unruh said, "I decided to shoot all of them so I would get the right one."[7]

He went to bed angry and got up around 8:00 A.M. to eat the breakfast of fried eggs that his mother had prepared. He then went into the basement to retrieve some items and returned. According to the statement Mrs. Unruh gave later, he seemed to go into a trance and when she probed to find out what was wrong, he spun around and held up a wrench as if he meant to hit her. So she left.

Unruh returned to his preparation. He figured that 9:30 was the time to begin, because most of the stores would be open. He could shoot everyone who had been talking about him. He had a 9-mm Luger purchased for $37.50 at M&H Sporting Goods in Philadelphia, and he had thirty-three rounds of ammunition. It was enough to do what he had in mind. He seemed to think no further than that and to be unaware that the law would catch up to him afterward. At just after nine o'clock, he had walked out into the neighborhood, fully armed.

As Unruh was being interrogated, no one noticed that he was bleeding until he rose from his seat. They sent him to Cooper Hospital, where he underwent surgery for his own wound, but surgeons were unable to remove the bullet. During that time, officials were asking a lot of questions about this man.

A check of Unruh's records indicated no report of mental illness before, during, or after his military service. He had an exemplary record
and those who knew him reported that he did not drink. No one at that
time knew much about posttraumatic stress syndrome, or even combat
fatigue. Few people—even the professionals—knew much about paranoid character disorders or schizophrenia.

Two psychiatrists, Drs. H. E. Yaskin and James Ryan, were assigned
to ask Unruh questions while he was still hospitalized at Cooper. It
seemed clear that he was destined for psychiatric treatment. Only a crazy
man, many said, would do what he had done. Yet his background was
unrevealing. Unruh seemed to have had an ordinary childhood, having
been a well-behaved boy, although reportedly he was quiet and moody.
He attended a Lutheran church every Sunday and studied the Bible. When
he was of age, he enlisted in the army in 1942 to fight for America during World War II, but most people did not realize that this was not just
a patriotic duty for him. It was also an experience that he painstakingly
documented.

He took excessive care of his rifle and was a brave soldier as a tank
gunner in Italy, Belgium, Austria, Germany, and France, taking part in
the relief of Bastogne in the Battle of the Bulge. Whenever he killed a
German, he wrote down the day, hour, and place. If he actually glimpsed
the remains, he described the corpse in some detail, shocking a fellow
soldier who read his diary. Unruh was honorably discharged in 1945 and
came home with medals for bravery and a collection of firearms. He
decorated his bedroom in the three-room apartment with military pieces.
On the walls he had hung pistols, machetes, German bayonets, and
photographs of armored artillery in action. Even his ashtrays were made
from German shells.

Unlike other solders, Unruh did not try to find a girlfriend and settle
down, although for a few weeks prior to his enlistment he had dated
a young woman who went to his church, but he had ended this relationship by letter from overseas. After coming home, he mostly remained inside his mother's apartment, becoming increasingly more
reclusive. She supported them both, although Howard had made and
sold a few model trains. For three months, he took pharmacy courses
at Temple University in Philadelphia. He also continued to attend
church and Bible classes.

A woman from his church who had corresponded with Howard when
he was overseas said that when he came back he was different. "He always appeared to be very nervous. He walked very straight on the street,
his head rigid, never glancing to the right or left." She thought he suffered from "war neurosis." Another church member who visited him a

month after he stopped going to church said that he exhibited strange behavior, believing that people were making things hard for him. This is precisely what Unruh's mother had been frightened about.

Unruh's brother, James, 25, said that Howard was a "born-again Christian" who had undergone a deep religious experience and had tried to live by the ways of Christ. Yet he'd become "nervous" over the past couple of months, according to statements James made to reporters. "He just seemed changed."[8]

Unruh's primary recreation had been collecting guns and target-shooting in the basement. Without a job, he just sat around the house, often thinking about what his neighbors were saying about him. He kept a list of grudges against them, imagining how he would get his revenge. Next to each offender's name he had recorded that person's misdeeds. Then he had written the word "retal," for retaliation. "I had been thinking about killing them for some time," Unruh commented. "I'd have killed a thousand if I'd had bullets enough."[9]

In summary, Howard Unruh appeared to be a quiet man who developed brooding suspicions but kept them to himself, letting them simmer and grow into paranoid delusions.

When he was able to leave Cooper Hospital, Unruh was sent to the New Jersey Hospital for the Insane (now Trenton Psychiatric Hospital), to be installed into a private cell in the maximum-security Vroom Building.

Prosecutor Cohen emphasized that the killer had not been declared insane, but that he would be receiving tests to determine his state of mind. It was not an involuntary admission by the court, but a voluntary agreement that four psychiatrists had recommended and Unruh had accepted. He'd asked to be subjected to further study and observation. Since he would need bed rest for at least two weeks anyway, the prosecutor had no reservations about leaving him in the hands of psychiatrists. He stated that it would benefit all concerned, but went ahead and filed the charges for thirteen "willful and malicious slayings with malice aforethought" and three counts of "atrocious assault and battery."

The tests were expected to take possibly as long as two months. During that time there were rumors that two of the four psychiatrists had determined that Unruh was sane. "He appears cognizant of his surroundings," said Dr. Dean Cavalli, a Camden-area physician, "and knows between right and wrong." But he added that he himself was not a psychiatrist. Nothing further was forthcoming.[10]

At the hospital, Dr. Robert S. Garber, assistant superintendent, and Dr. James Spradley began their assessments, attended by the prosecutor and several detectives. News photographers were permitted to enter the isolation cell for pictures. Unruh submitted without expression. Reportedly, Unruh was surprised by the treatment he was receiving, and commented that it was better than he deserved. He expressed some remorse over dropping out of pharmacy courses, because he could have devoted himself to saving lives. No one records him expressing remorse about the victims.

Dr. Edward Strecker, of the medical school of the University of Pennsylvania and a consultant for the armed services, told reporters that war does not cause an increase in the number of actual cases of insanity. Strecker believed that Unruh's illness must have built up over the years—a prescient comment in light of what we now know about mass murderers. The type of killing that he had undertaken could not be traced to military service. The war had simply provided the opportunity to learn to use the weapons. Although he had not examined Unruh himself, Strecker thought the man had just gone "gun crazy."

Another psychiatrist, unidentified, thought that Unruh's overtly religious character might have given him a savior complex, and that Unruh, when he saw that he had failed to save the world, reacted out of disappointment in himself.

This incident, as with all future such events, brought out a number of theories about what had caused the violence. No one had clear answers, although many would make pronouncements that they did. During that time, Unruh made comments to the effect that he believed he would be electrocuted for his crimes, but he did not seem disturbed by the idea.

While they awaited the official results, reporters looked around for earlier signs of Unruh's mental instability. The Woodrow Wilson High School yearbook from 1939 indicated that he was shy and that his ambition was to become a government employee (as would be the ambition of many shooters of the future). They called him "How." A check of his records revealed Bs and Cs for things like "health," "courtesy," and "personal impression." There was no evaluation of his intelligence, but his mental alertness was average. Most people thought he was "nice."

After a month of personality and physiological tests, the assessment by four board-certified psychiatrists was concluded and their collective report was issued on October 8, 1949. Prosecutor Mitchell Cohen announced it to the press. A commission had found that Unruh had "Dementia praecox, mixed type, with pronounced catatonic and paranoid coloring." (Reporters interpreted this as a guilt complex coupled with delusions of persecution.) In other words, Unruh was considered a paranoid schizophrenic, caught in a world of his own delusions and separated from reality. His mental illness had come upon him slowly and was not caused by combat. He was considered insane and would be formally committed to a psychiatric institution.

"After careful consideration of all the facts involved," the report read, "with particular attention to the medico-legal implications, it is our opinion that this man should be regularly committed to Trenton State Hospital, where custody, supervision, and treatment is available and people in the community will be protected from injury or danger should there be a recurrence of his homicidal impulses."[11]

Pronounced insane, Unruh was immune from criminal prosecution. He was sentenced for the remainder of his life to the Vroom Building, the unit for the criminally insane. His father, separated from his mother and at the time a cook on a dredge, was ordered to pay $15 a week for his maintenance in the gray, 8-foot-by-10-foot cell. Newspapers reported that it was on the first floor, and from his iron-barred window he had a spectacular view.

One reporter for the *Philadelphia Inquirer* indicated that the psychiatrists had left open a legal loophole. Their report indicated that Unruh was insane at the time of their examination but no one mentioned his mental state at the time of the offense. So he could conceivably have been prosecuted. But mass murder was such a rare incident at the time that few people thought much about this aspect. Decades later, this difference between present mental state and mental state when an offense was committed would become more of a legal issue in mass murder. At the time, it seemed pretty clear that someone who did such a thing was seriously mentally unstable.

Unruh himself resisted the idea that he was insane, and his behaviors bear this out, at least in the legal sense. When he heard sirens, he rushed home. Thus he knew that what he had done was illegal or wrong. He was aware of his behavior and he had made a plan. That frame of mind, which shows an understanding of the difference between right and wrong, generally indicates sanity in today's courts.

Relatives of the victims were outraged. Some wanted him to be not only executed but also tortured for what he had done to their loved ones. One reporter noted that despite promises made by the prosecutor that Unruh would never be a free man, in Chicago at that time, Nathan Leopold, who had been sentenced to life for the murder of a child, was about to clear the last legal hurdle to gaining his freedom (which he in fact accomplished). Yet unlike Leopold, who had gone through a rather sensational trial, Unruh, were he found harmless enough by psychiatrists to be released, could legally be tried for the crimes and returned to prison.

Dr. Richard Noll, professor of psychology at DeSales University, author of *The Encyclopedia of Schizophrenia and the Psychotic Disorders*, and historian of psychiatry, offered a perspective on the manner in which Unruh may have been diagnosed in 1949. After reviewing the case details, he believed that the likely diagnosis was a schizoid or paranoid personality disorder. "When someone was violent back then," he pointed out, "they always invoked the diagnosis of paranoid schizophrenia. If someone was distraught (from emotional trauma, for example), that might be called 'pseudo-neurotic schizophrenia.'"

He went on to say that paranoid schizophrenia has traditionally been one of the most misused diagnostic labels in both clinical and forensic contexts. Schizophrenia is a chronic brain disease that takes many forms. The age of onset for the paranoid subtype tends to be slightly older than for other subtypes. The hallmark of the paranoid subtype is delusions of a persecutory or grandiose nature. For Unruh, the violent incident would have to be understood within the context of prior mental status and subsequent clinical observations. "Anyone," he said, "especially a male under great stress due to a divorce, job loss, death of a loved one, etc., could become paranoid and violent under conditions of extreme and prolonged stress."

Yet Noll indicated that it is difficult to distinguish among paranoid schizophrenia, an agitated manic episode of bipolar disorder, delusional disorder, a brief psychotic reaction, and someone with a paranoid personality disorder who simply loses control and acts out. "The diagnostic criteria for paranoid schizophrenia have tightened up considerably since the 1940s when this incident took place, and back then the term paranoid schizophrenia was liberally dispensed in a forensic context as almost a euphemism for 'raving madman.' Anytime violence entered the case history, the 'paranoid schizophrenia' diagnostic label was almost automatically applied, even if someone was bipolar and violent, or under stress and violent."[12]

In other words, had Unruh gone on his rampage today, his paranoia would have been acknowledged, but unless psychosis (i.e., hallucinations) actually affected his ability to appreciate that what he was doing was wrong or made him unable to comply with what he knew, then he would have been declared legally sane. There was nothing about his demeanor that would have prevented him from being in court, and if he could have assisted in his own defense, he would have been deemed competent to stand trial.

Howard Unruh remained at Trenton Psychiatric Hospital and as of this writing is still there, taking walks and mopping floors. Now in his 80s, he reportedly has spoken to no one since his mother died some years ago. He has ground privileges now and just keeps to himself.

The headlines were past and the case was over. Twelve minutes, thirteen lives. As scary as it had been for those people in the neighborhood, it had been contained and was likely just an aberrant event. Or so people may have thought back then.

MORE MASSACRES

The next year, 1950, in Piney Hollow, New Jersey, Ernest Ingenito shot and killed five people and wounded four others, but it appeared to have been the result of a family squabble, and most of the victims were his relatives. That same year in Texas, William Cook also shot and killed five members of his family.

Then five years passed and the next mass murder astonished the county, in terms of both victim count and modus operandi. In Colorado on November 1, 1955, John Graham, 23, placed a bomb on United Airlines flight 629, according to Brian Lane and Wilfred Gregg in *The Encyclopedia of Mass Murder*. The bomb brought down the plane, and with it forty-four people, ten minutes into its flight. His design, Graham said during his confession, had been to kill his mother, Daisy King, a passenger on the plane. He hated her and wanted her insurance money, to the tune of $62,000. He was convicted and executed for this crime.

Four years later, in 1959 in Texas, Paul H. Orgeron reacted in anger against the difficulty he was having getting his 7-year-old son enrolled in Houston's Poe Elementary School, so he brought a bomb to the playground. Someone tried to get it from him, but it exploded and killed Orgeron, his son, two other children, a teacher, and a custodian, and injured twenty—two so seriously that their legs had to be amputated. People who knew Orgeron had no explanation for why he had done this, aside from his need for control.

No one expected these kinds of incidents to increase in number and define a type of killer, let alone divide into subtypes, but as the 1950s evolved into the 1960s, America would witness a startling new era, one that would force criminologists and psychologists to learn about them and attempt to educate the public. It began with a spree killing in 1957–58 and a massacre in 1959 that would make people around the country feel vulnerable to random, senseless attacks.

CHAPTER 2

Buildup to Horror

SPREE VS. MASS

On December 1, 1957, 19-year-old Charles Starkweather held up a gas station, abducting the attendant and driving him into the countryside to shoot him in the head. Six weeks later, Starkweather shot and killed the parents of his girlfriend, Caril Ann Fugate, and murdered her 2-year-old sister. Fugate stayed with him, apparently without question, and they took off. He next killed a family friend and a pair of recently engaged teenagers who gave them a ride. He forced this couple into a storm cellar and shot them. Then Starkweather and Fugate invaded a home and murdered an older couple and their deaf maid. Their final act before these two marauders were caught was to kill a man for his car. The details can be found in Michael Newton's *Waste Land.*

At this point, no one had yet made a distinction between a mass murderer and a spree killer. There just weren't a sufficient number of cases of either to begin to understand where lay the differences; it would be over two decades before that occurred. But the community that experienced the killings was just as stunned. Starkweather and Fugate were caught and held for separate trials.

Due to the shockingly explosive nature of their crimes, and with the death penalty impending, Dr. James M. Reinhardt, professor of criminology at the University of Nebraska, spent about thirty hours interviewing Starkweather before making his report. In his book, *The Murderous Trail of Charles Starkweather,* he described the killer as having a suspicious, unrealistic assessment of the world around him. The third of seven children, he'd grown up in abject poverty, and he was short, myopic, redheaded, bowlegged, and had a speech impediment. Taunted by classmates as "Red Headed Peckerwood," he lapsed into black moods, developing an intense hatred against those who humiliated him. Thus far, he is not unlike Unruh. When in 1956 he watched James Dean play a nihilistic adolescent named Jim Stark in the film *Rebel Without a Cause*, Starkweather found his hero.

There was no apparent abuse in his background and his murderous rage seemed rooted in the cruelties inflicted on him by peers, along with his inability to forgive them and move on. For Starkweather, the world had become an intolerable place and his symbol of power was the gun. Again, in this respect he is similar to Unruh.

When Starkweather went on trial, his attorney attempted to show that he could not have premeditated those killings, because he either was insane or had an organic brain disorder. Other psychiatrists who assessed him said that Starkweather had a paranoid assessment of the world, a consuming hatred, and a delusional quality to his responses. Since he'd given several different versions of what he and Fugate had done, they interpreted this as a "processing disorder." In short, they felt that he was not entirely responsible for his actions.

The jury rejected the expert opinion about his diminished capacity, and Starkweather was found guilty and sentenced to die. But what he and Fugate had done in attacking strangers along the way had alerted the people to a pervasive sense of vulnerability. If a mass killer starts traveling, and even walks into homes, anyone could become a target.

Right afterward came an apparently random assault on an ordinary midwestern family, the Herbert Clutter family in Holcomb, Kansas. It was one thing for a crazed family member to kill those to whom he was related. That was bad enough, but for strangers to commit such slaughter made people wonder what the country was coming to.

While the Clutter family massacre was a local occurrence, it warranted a few paragraphs in New York papers, grabbing the attention of a writer named Truman Capote. He immortalized this incident in his original work of narrative nonfiction *In Cold Blood*, offering an intensely detailed study of the team of killers who had committed it.

On November 15, 1959, in search of money at the farmhouse owned by Herbert Clutter, Dick Hickock and Perry Smith slaughtered all four members of the family and then made a run for it.

Hickock, a psychopathic drifter from a stable home, had met Smith in prison. Smith suffered from a bad leg, limited intelligence, and serious headaches. He'd bragged that he'd once murdered a man, so Dick thought he could use Perry to pull off the murder of this rich farmer whom he'd heard about from a fellow con. Herb Clutter, 48, supposedly had a safe full of money—$10,000—and it would be easy pickings for a man who knew where to go. Dick had a plan, and when he and Perry were released, he put it into motion.

As they collected the things they would need, Dick reportedly insisted that there be no witnesses. They were to leave no one alive. Perry wasn't so sure, but he didn't argue. They moved on to the farmhouse. Waiting one evening until the place looked dark, they entered, cut the phone lines, and roused Clutter out of bed. Tying up his wife and two adolescent children in various rooms, they demanded he open the safe. Clutter insisted there was no safe. That's when the burglars became upset. They had planned this meticulously, they were in financial straits, and they'd spun fantasies about what they would do when they got rich. This stubborn resistance was not part of the plan. One by one, in separate areas of the house, the two men killed each member of the family.

When the Clutters missed church services the next morning, friends went to find out what was wrong. This behavior was clearly out of character. The murderous rampage from the night before was soon discovered.

Nancy Clutter, 16, was found first. She had been shot in the back of the head at close range. She was lying on her side, facing a wall that was covered in a spray of blood. Her hands and ankles were bound, but the covers had been pulled over her. On the same floor, Mrs. Clutter was on her bed, shot dead, with her hands tied in front of her. Her mouth had been taped with adhesive and her eyes were wide open in terrible fear. But there was no sign of Kenyon or Herb Clutter.

The investigators went into the basement, where they quickly discovered young Kenyon lying on a couch, his head cradled on a pillow, bound hand and foot with tape over his mouth. He'd been shot squarely in the face, at close range. It was a horrific sight, but not as bad as the condition of the final victim.

Herb was sprawled on a mattress box in front of the furnace. He, too, had been shot in the face, but his throat had been cut as well. Tape was wound around his head and across his mouth, and his ankles were tied together. Next to him was the bloodstained imprint of a shoe or boot.

No one had any idea who could have done this. Clutter had no enemies in town. But neighbors began locking their doors, wondering at what lay inside the hearts of people they thought they knew. Then investigators learned about a man in the Kansas state penitentiary who had told Hickock about Clutter—the man who'd described the nonexistent safe. He believed he knew who had killed the Clutter family, and he'd confided his secret to a fellow inmate, who then told the warden.

The search was on, with eighteen men from various law enforcement agencies assigned to the case.

Hickock and Smith were arrested in Las Vegas after they had traveled from Mexico to Acapulco to Miami Beach, and back to the Southwest. They were brought to Garden City, Kansas. After a trial, they were convicted. Over the next five years, as their appeals went through the courts, Capote got to know Smith rather well. Ironically, Smith said that all he'd ever wanted to do in his life was to produce a work of art, and now his crime was going to do that for him. He didn't like the title, though. The murders, he insisted, were not committed in cold blood. He added that he had nothing against the Clutters. They hadn't done anything to him, but they were the ones who had to pay. In other words, for a lifetime of bad luck and poor treatment, Smith had simply acted out against those for whom life had seemed good.

It was never quite clear which man had committed the murders. Hickock, who was the first to break down and confess, denied committing any of them, but Smith said that he'd done two and then had handed Hickock the rifle and told him to finish it. So that was two apiece. But then Smith changed the story. He had no living parents and Hickock did, so he said he didn't mind taking the full rap. Both men were tried and sentenced to be hanged.

Such team killers are often guided by a central figure with a particular fantasy, and something about his energy inspires the other participants to serve that fantasy. To some degree, all willing partners have psychopathic traits, and while a few have claimed after arrest to have been unwilling accomplices, the evidence indicates otherwise. Quite often the willing partner is schizotypal, a personality disorder that renders them unstable, eccentric, easily manipulated, and even superstitious.

Yet even as a team, Hickock and Smith expressed sentiments similar to those of mass murderers like Unruh. The world has been unfair, and they were going to even the score. They didn't much care who would get hurt. However, unlike Unruh, who suffered from some mental disturbance, Hickock was more likely a cold-hearted psychopath who was merely attempting to enrich himself rather than seeking revenge or making a statement. He had a plan for escape and for leaving the country. He did not wish to be killed or caught in the process. He and Smith are the precursors to another, rarer type of mass murderer—the person who kills to eliminate witnesses or out of anger created within the situation itself, not from some long-standing grudge.

It was Richard Speck who made the next set of headlines around the country, and his crime would have an internal landscape entirely different from any seen before.

SEXUAL FRENZY

Students often share quarters to help with expenses, and such was the case with the eight nurses who lived in a townhouse at 2319 East 100th Street in Chicago, and whose activities may have come to the attention of a deeply disturbed man: Richard Speck, a man who felt sure that he was destined to one day shock the world.

He was suspected in several murders in different states, but on those investigations he had always managed to stay a step ahead of the law. Born on December 6, 1941, into a family of eight children in Kirkwood, Illinois, he had been a sickly child. At age 5, he suffered a severe head injury from a hammer and the following year he fell out of a tree. Later, he ran into an awning, which resulted in severe repetitive headaches, and suffered another accident that resulted in yet another head injury.

When his father died, his mother took him and his sister to Dallas, Texas. Richard was 5, and his life was now spent with these two females. Then his mother married an ex-con and Speck grew to resent her and her new husband. Some criminologists suggest that he felt betrayed and thus the seeds of his anger toward women began to grow.

Full of internal rage against the world, the sulky boy began drinking around age 12 and from that time on was frequently in trouble with the law for various infractions. When he flunked the ninth grade, he dropped out. He suffered from fierce headaches that he claimed made him drink even more, and he often added drugs to the mix.

When he was 18, he beat up his mother. He was developing the attitude that women did not deserve to be treated well, because they always disappointed. Nevertheless, when he was 20, he marred Shirley Annette Malone, a 15-year-old. After they had a baby, Speck tattooed the female child's name on his arm. Yet he could not hold down a job or his relationship, and his marriage quickly failed.

Speck liked to express his ideas on his body, and he sported many tattoos along his arms and torso: a serpent coiled around a dagger, an inscription, "Born to Raise Hell." One tattoo bore the names "Richard and Shirley," which he had tried to scrape off. He also developed an affection for knives and carried one around with him. When he was drunk, he was especially mean.

Speck spent several years in prison, one term of which was for assault on a woman with a knife. During that time, Shirley filed for divorce. Speck vowed revenge. To his mind, she was no better than a cheating spouse. She remarried quickly, confirming his suspicion that she had betrayed him. He was fiercely angry at his ex-wife to the point of blind hate.

Speck returned to Illinois, where he still had family, though he vowed to return to Texas one day to kill his wife. Around that time, another woman whom he had encountered disappeared and was found murdered.

Landing a job on a barge, his drinking got him into trouble. In one town where he ended up, three women disappeared. Whether he was responsible was never known, but suspicions ran high.

Speck returned to Chicago to figure out what to do. His siblings gave him a hand, but he seemed destined to go downhill—which for him was not very far. He took a room in a flophouse and found a job, only to learn that he'd lost it before it had even begun. Frustrated and angry, he started to drink. He then took some drugs—sodium seconals. That day, July 13, 1966, he drank throughout most of the afternoon. Then he took a walk.

It may be true that he was bent only on robbery, but it may also be true that he had seen the women who lived at 2319 East 100th Street, which was not far from the Maritime Union Hall, a job-posting association for seamen that he visited each day. The evidence seems to indicate that he had some idea of what he was getting into. Entering the nurses' home through a ground-level kitchen window around 11:00 P.M., he went to a bedroom door on the second floor and rapped sharply four times. Corazon Amurao, awakened from sleep, answered the door.

Five American senior nursing students and three Filipino graduate nurses lived there. All were in their early 20s. Six were home at the time, one of whom was a friend who occasionally stayed there. Three were still out.

When Amurao started to open the door, Speck pushed his way in, holding a gun trained directly at her. He told her and the other woman in the room to stay there and then he searched two other bedrooms on that floor, where he found the four other women. He made them join Amurao and her roommate. One asked him what he wanted, and he reportedly told them that he was there for money. They readily gave him all they had. Nevertheless, he used his knife to cut the sheets into strips to bind the wrists of the women. He ignored their requests to explain himself, but he remained friendly and reassuring. He sat on the floor, smoking and telling them that he was bound for New Orleans. Then something shifted.

A woman who lived there, Gloria Davy, an attractive American, came home from her date. Speck met her downstairs and immediately took her up to the room to place her with the others. Amurao later said that Speck's demeanor completely changed. Many experts on mass murder or criminal behavior have speculated that because Davy so strongly resembled Speck's former wife, Shirley, she triggered his anger.

Then the doorbell rang again, and Speck forced two women to accompany him to let whomever was there inside. The women still in the room remained where they were, probably hoping that it would all be over soon and that he would take what he wanted and leave. But no one was at the door—and it turned out later that another student had come by to borrow something but left when no one answered.

Speck went upstairs to finish binding Davy. Now he had seven captives. He sat on the floor, asking odd questions and growing more agitated. Their concern turned to fear. They had no idea what he intended. He kept looking at Davy. Then he stood up, as if to leave. Instead, he untied Pamela Wilkening's ankles and led her out alone. She spat on him, which may have been a deciding factor in what he would do. He indicated as much many years later in a prison video, saying that she had threatened him with identification in a lineup. The others heard her make a sound like a sigh and then all was quiet. They were not sure what had just taken place.

The other two women who lived in the townhouse arrived home and came up the steps. Speck took them to the south bedroom. But then he forced them back out again. The bound women heard muffled screams and sounds of a struggle. Then, after silence, they heard water running in the bathroom. Speck later said he was killing off witnesses. He appeared once more at the door. He looked around and selected another woman, Nina Schmale. She, too, made an odd sighing noise and within twenty minutes Speck was back.

Some of the women tried to hide under the beds, but Speck pulled them out and took them away. By this time, the survivors knew they were all going to be killed. They didn't know what to do, and so he took them, one by one. Speck later said he'd used a knife on them because it was quieter than a gun. At least one of the women was also strangled with the strips of a sheet, and another was kicked hard in the stomach.

When only Davy and Amurao were left, Speck came in and turned his attention on Davy. Amurao had managed to maneuver herself under a bed. She listened as Speck prepared Davy for rape and then watched from her hiding place as he positioned the woman. He raped her for about twenty minutes and then took her outside the room.

Amurao waited for his final visit. But he did not come. Several hours went by as she tried to free herself. She heard an alarm ring, which had been set to awaken someone for her morning shift. The house was otherwise silent. Still, she waited. She did not want to let the man know she was there.

Finally it became clear to her that the intruder had overlooked her. He might even have left or fallen asleep. She had to get out and get help.

Cautiously listening and peering about, she saw in the other bedrooms what she had feared: the eight nurses had all been stabbed or strangled to death, some bearing more wounds than others. One had been stabbed through her eye.

Not daring to go downstairs, lest Speck was still there, she stepped over three bodies—one of which lay on top of another—to push out a window from the front bedroom and scream, "Help me! They are all dead! My friends are all dead!"

A neighbor who saw her alerted the police and the first responding officer came in to find a body on the living room couch. The victim had been raped, sodomized, and strangled. It was Gloria Davy.

Upstairs, they found the other seven victims. Gasping through her terror, Amurao gave the police a description of the man who had done this and they sent it out to units everywhere in the vicinity. She could not tell them how long ago he had left.

A drawing of the intruder was published in newspapers, under blaring headlines about the massacre. The man had blue eyes, a pockmarked face, light-colored hair, and a tattoo that read "Born to Raise Hell." At the Maritime Union Hall, the police learned about a man by that description who had been inquiring about jobs. They soon discovered his name: Richard Speck, age 24. They lured him to the hall via his sister with the promise of a job, and he bit. But then he did not show up for his appointment. Acquiring a photo of Speck from Coast Guard files, they showed it to Amurao and she made a positive identification. Fingerprints from the house matched his as well. They knew who they were looking for.

In the meantime, Speck hired a prostitute and the police actually encountered him when a motel manager called them about problems, but they did not yet know that this was the man they were seeking. For his part, Speck did not yet seem to realize he was being sought.

On July 15, 1966, he heard a radio announcement about the murders and made a comment that someone heard and later remembered to the effect that he hoped they caught the son of a bitch. The next day, his name was in the press. Speck heard about this and bought himself a bottle of wine. Checking into a flophouse, he lay on the grubby mattress and got drunk. Then he slashed his right wrist in a suicide attempt, but directly afterward sought assistance. Under his bed lay a Chicago newspaper that bore the headline "Police Say Nurse Survivor Can Identify Slayer of 8."

The police actually took Speck to a local hospital without realizing who they were escorting. The attending doctor recognized the man from the papers, looked for the tattoo, and turned him in. Amurao confirmed that he was the man who had killed all of her roommates.

Speck denied his part in the murders and entered a plea of not guilty in court. He said he did not remember anything after an evening of drinking and claimed that a stranger had given him an injection of speed. He was clearly attempting to use amnesia as his defense—a ploy that had worked for him in the past when arrested for another crime. While awaiting trial, he took a correspondence course in Bible study and received a certificate that he had passed. He was proud of that.

The trial was moved to Peoria, as if a change of venue would make some difference. Speck showed only boredom throughout the proceedings. Based mostly on thirty-three fingerprints from the crime scene and the strength of Amurao's defiant testimony against him, Speck was quickly convicted. The jury recommended death.

He may well have been executed, save for a moratorium on the death penalty declared by the U.S. Supreme Court in 1972. He was sentenced at that time to eight consecutive terms of life imprisonment. He served his time at the Statesville Correctional Center at Joliet, Illinois, and in ten years he became eligible for parole. In 1978 he admitted to a reporter from the *Chicago Tribune*, "Yeah, I killed them. I stabbed them and choked them."[1]

He also became one of the subjects for study by the FBI's budding Behavioral Science Unit (BSU), which conducted prison interviews to build up an offender database. In *Mindhunter*, former special agent and BSU chief John Douglas describes his own interview with Speck, who was reluctant to talk. But Speck did say that he had raped Gloria Davy, but none of the others. Douglas had heard a story that Speck had made a pet out of a sparrow, but that when he was told he could not have it, he threw it to its death into a fan, saying that no one else could have it either. In other words, he cared only about himself.

Former special agent Robert Ressler, another of those who interviewed Speck, said that the multiple offender had no insight into his behavior. "Speck displayed a callousness for human life," Ressler writes in *Whoever Fights Monsters*, "admitting that he had killed his victims so they couldn't testify against him."[2]

In years to come, Speck would claim that he did not know why he massacred the women. Psychiatrist Marvin Ziporyn, who saw Speck at least twice a week and later penned the book about him (with Jack Altman) *Born to Raise Hell*, said that Speck showed many signs that indicated brain damage: he had the IQ of a 10-year-old, had acted out in sporadic compulsive rages, and had experienced numerous head injuries. He had also suffered from oxygen deprivation as an infant. He was impulsive, willful, rigid, and self-centered like a child, and reported having blackouts. Ziporyn believed that his mother's coddling as Speck grew up only exacerbated his immaturity. He was never asked to take responsibility for himself.

Speck also supposedly had what Ziporyn labeled the "Madonna-Whore Complex," viewing women within only two rigid stereotypes: having untouchable perfection or being flagrant sluts. Anyone—including a wife—who had sex with him was automatically relegated to the latter category, even if he forced it. He did finally admit that Gloria Davy, the nurse whom he had so viciously raped and mutilated before killing, was a dead ringer for his ex-wife, and that Davy had made him angry. Ziporyn speculated that her physical appearance had triggered a rage that had snapped Speck's already eroding inhibitions that day.

Other psychiatrists believed that Speck was an outright psychopath, feeling sorrier for himself than for anything he had done. He displayed this with his casual attitude about the crimes. Yet Ziporyn was certain that Speck had a conscience.

One day shy of his 50th birthday, in 1991, Richard Speck died in prison of a heart attack. His remains were cremated. He had been repeatedly rejected for parole, but he had not seemed to mind. A clandestine film of some of his prison activities, discovered in 1996, indicated that he seemed right at home. He was still getting drunk and taking drugs, but oddly enough he had taken on the persona of a woman. The film shows him with large breasts and a flabby body, dressed in silky bikini briefs and acting as a sex object for other men. Through this gimmick, he received favors and gifts from other prisoners. In this film, he said that after killing the nurses, he had no feelings at all. He did not feel sorry. When asked for a reason, he said, "It just wasn't their night."[3] He indicated that Gloria Davy had been flirting with him.

Dr. Ziporyn, upon viewing Speck in the video, indicated that he believed that Speck had punished himself for the crimes by forfeiting his manhood and being used and humiliated by other men in the same way in which he had performed similar degradation on women. Some indication of this remorse, for Ziporyn, was found in Speck's repeated attempts to scrape off the macho snake tattoo that had betrayed him.

The idea of an intruder like Richard Speck invading one's own home in this manner and doing what he did hit Americans hard. Throughout the 1950s and into the early 1960s, before racial riots and college protests, people generally felt safe. They had the impression that if they did the right things, their lives would work out well. But Speck's victims had been nurses—good women who were making a contribution to society. It did not make sense. Speck's massacre was one more sign that social erosion was occurring and no one could stop it and the damage it could cause.

Speck was not the only mass murderer to commit his crime in combination with a sexual assault. In 1989, Ramon Salcido turned on his family and coworkers in northern California, killing seven and injuring three, as well as molesting two of them. He, too, had felt rejected and had wanted revenge. He also had relied on drugs (cocaine in this case) and alcohol, and had harbored a developing hatred against all women. On April 14, he killed his boss and wounded a coworker at a winery. Then he shot his 24-year-old wife. He grabbed his three young daughters and from there went to the home of his mother-in-law, where he killed her and raped and sodomized her two daughters. He shot and killed them before turning his murderous anger on his own children. He cut their throats and tossed them onto a garbage heap. Two died but one survived to finger her father.

Upon his capture, he said that he had done it all because he suspected his wife was cheating on him. While he might be more accurately labeled as a family killer than as resembling someone like Speck, who murdered outright strangers, the sexual assault during the murders gives him common ground with the notorious Speck. In other words, Speck was a prototype, not a unique entity.

The debate over the type of disorder a mass murderer may have generally takes one of three directions: he (or she) is organically impaired, psychotic, or psychopathic. The cases explored in the next chapter raise each of these issues. Although the shaken Chicago coroner who examined Speck's victims had called the killer's murderous sexual frenzy "the crime of the century," he could not have known then that a worse bloodbath was only two weeks away.

CHAPTER 3

The Classic Mass Murderer

MYG ATTACK

The clock tower at the University of Texas at Austin stands over three hundred feet high. It's the first thing travelers notice on the otherwise flat landscape as they fly into the city. From its observation deck is a 360-degree view of the campus and city. It was from this spot, writes Gary Lavergne in *A Sniper in the Tower*, where Charles Joseph Whitman, 25, decided to shoot people at random on August 1, 1966. The nation was only just recovering from the horror in Chicago that Richard Speck had perpetrated, and now another area of the country was under attack. This time, it was more spectacular and even deadlier.

It was nearly 11:30 A.M. when Whitman came onto the campus, using the pretense of delivering something to a professor. This gave him a parking space close to the university's administration building. In his car was a footlocker full of supplies and survival gear, and in the trunk a virtual arsenal: rifles, shotguns, a carbine, two pistols, a revolver, and ammunition.

"Terrorism" was not yet a word in common use, but this man would introduce the experience to students, shoppers, workers, and tourists in Austin on that hot summer day. People would learn what it meant to be attacked for no good reason, by a stranger, suddenly, and with devastating effect.

Whitman used a wheeled dolly to haul his heavy load into a service elevator. A helpful employee switched it on for him so he could get to the twenty-seventh floor. From there he hauled his trunk and weaponry up to the observation deck on the thirtieth floor. He encountered a female greeter and hit her with the butt of a shotgun, splitting her skull. Then he shot her and hid her unconscious body. He was on a mission. A young couple barely escaped the same fate as they made their hasty exit.

Whitman blocked the door to the stairs, but then two boys tried to get in. Whitman fired at them with a spray of pellets. The boys tumbled back against relatives coming up behind them. Two people died and two others were critically wounded. The survivors dragged the injured to safety. Now workers in the building were alert to some sort of emergency, although they had no idea what was happening.

Whitman went to the observation deck, wedged his dolly against the door to keep people out, and prepared for his ultimate event. His fortress was ready. He stood under the gilt-edged clock's south face, looking around. He did not expect to survive this day's dark work.

Classes had let out and many students were walking across the paved campus mall. Whitman watched them, but it was too late for him to take full advantage. The delay caused by running into those people had cost him. There were fewer people walking across the green than he had expected. Still, there were enough. He could not turn back now. At 11:48, Whitman lifted the scoped 6-mm Remington, aimed, and pulled the trigger. Once, twice, again and again. Across a four-block area, people began to fall to the ground.

No one knew what was happening. They heard shots, screams; they saw people looking around or falling. Several who looked up spotted smoke from the tower, but could not interpret what it meant, or the popping sounds coming from that direction. It was mass confusion. Now six bodies were sprawled on the mall. Then several more people fell, bleeding from their wounds.

Whitman used handguns to continue. A pregnant woman was shot in the abdomen. The fetus's skull was crushed, killing it. Someone who helped her was shot dead. Another man was hit in the back, and a secretary who went to assist people had to take cover as she watched others being mowed down. A police officer arrived to assess the scene, but he was killed before he could figure out what to do.

Five hundred yards away, an electrical repairman was killed with a bullet to the stomach. In another direction, as the shooter turned and pulled the trigger, a student bound for the Peace Corps was killed. Whitman looked from one side of the campus to another. Protected from nearly any angle, he picked out his targets carefully. Moving from students to nearby shoppers, he aimed again and fired. An 18-year-old boy and his girlfriend were killed together. Not far from there, a father of six fell to the sidewalk, as did a student walking back from an exam.

People who were lying on the ground, wounded, were scared to get up and run for fear of being hit again, so they crouched down against the steaming sidewalk, feeling the burn of the concrete as well as the agony of their wounds and wondering if they might die before they got help.

Police officers converged on the campus, coming in waves. Over 130 personnel responded. Some residents came running with their private weapons to assist as well. People began to shoot at the tower. Bullets hit the clock but did not take down the well-protected shooter. He moved out of range and used slits in the wall to continue his rampage. They couldn't touch him up there. He continued to shoot and wounded two more students. Then he shot again and killed several more.

By that time, the police had flown an aircraft into range to try to come at the shooter from above, even as they put themselves in harm's way. They felt the impact of his shots and hoped the plane would not go down. They could not get close enough to stop him.

Yet their efforts deflected Whitman's attention from the campus, allowing three police officers and a deputized civilian to run quickly and get into the building to make their way up the stairs. They intended to storm the tower. They had no idea what they would face. It could be one shooter, it could be several. As they climbed, they encountered the dead and wounded family, moved past them, and kept going. Then they found the barriers and the first person who had been attacked. Alerted to the madman's frenzy, they made their way to the glass door that led out to the deck. Now they could clearly hear the shooter at his deadly work. The police officers jumped forward and surrounded a blond man on the deck, who had a radio tuned to the news. He turned and aimed at the officers moving toward him, but they got him first, right in the head. He went down. The threat was vanquished.

To make sure, they shot him six times before they approached. It was 1:24 P.M.—around ninety-six minutes had passed since the first shot was fired. A man signaled from the tower with a towel to the people below that the rampage was over. Fourteen people lay dead, and thirty were critically wounded.

Investigators soon learned that there were more bodies elsewhere. The night before his rampage, Whitman had stabbed his mother and shot her in the head. Then he had left a typed note: "If there's a heaven, she's going there. If there is not a heaven, she is out of her pain and misery." Then he went home. Around three o'clock that morning, he went to the bedroom and stabbed his sleeping wife three times in the chest with a bayonet. He indicated that he wanted to spare her the embarrassment of what he was planning to do.

Those who knew him could not believe that he was the person who had done this awful deed. Mostly, they described him with such adjectives as "nice," "dependable," "uncomplicated," and "normal." He loved children and "was a great guy." He'd given no sign that he was pondering an act so violent and deadly. People well acquainted with him were utterly stymied. Nevertheless, his background did yield some foreboding signals.

Born on June 24, 1941, Whitman had grown up the eldest of three sons in Lake Worth, Florida, with middle-class, Catholic values and experiences. He was an altar boy, a newspaper boy, and an eagle scout, but his father, a plumber, had a bad temper, demanded a lot, and frequently assaulted his wife. He was also a gun fanatic, and he taught his two sons how to hunt. Whitman became an expert shot.

At age 18, after a humiliating beating by his father, Charles Whitman joined the marines, showing the streak of anger he shared with his father. He became a fine marksman, and then earned a military scholarship for university courses. He looked like an all-American young man, and made friends easily, but rage smoldered beneath the surface. He married a woman named Kathy Leissner in 1962 and began taking classes at the University of Texas at Austin in mechanical and architectural engineering. He did not do well, uncharacteristically, and was then called back into the marines. Soon he was sentenced to hard labor for aggression and committing some petty crimes, and his rank was reduced to private.

In 1964 he wrote in his diary about feelings that he might explode. He mentioned to several friends that he had ideas about shooting people from the Texas tower, but no one took him seriously. He apparently told no one why he would consider such a thing. That year, Whitman was honorably discharged from the marines, so he took on a job and a large load of courses. He also passed a licensure exam to become a real estate broker. To pump up his energy, he began taking amphetamines.

Whitman's mother left his father in the spring of 1966, so Charles helped her move to Austin, where he lived. Around that time, he dropped out of school and told his wife that he was leaving her. She asked why, but he could not give a reason. Kathy was afraid of him, since, following in the footsteps of his father, he'd been beating her. He apparently told her that the stresses of life were becoming overwhelming. Kathy persuaded him to see a psychiatrist.

On March 29, 1966, he went to see Dr. Maurice Dean Heatly, the staff psychiatrist at the university health center, to talk about his rage. He was not feeling like himself, he admitted, and he thought he might snap. He had experienced periods of hostility that had seemed unprovoked. He even described his fantasy of going up onto the tower and shooting people. The psychiatrist urged him to return for more sessions, but he decided not to. Instead, he nurtured his rage—aiming a lot of it at his father. He also complained of debilitating headaches, and on July 31 he decided to record his thoughts. "I am prepared to die," he wrote. He wondered if he was mentally ill. He thought he might have to kill his wife. Oddly, he asked in this note that, upon his death, an autopsy be performed to determine if he had a disorder.

While he was writing this note, some friends stopped by. They later said that nothing about him that evening seemed out of the ordinary, but admitted that Whitman had seemed agitated during the days prior to their visit. When they left, he went to pick up his wife from her job and took her home. Then he drove across town to where his mother lived to kill her. He returned home to kill Kathy and prepare his weapons and rations for the morning's rampage.

A friend saw Whitman before he went into the tower and thought he looked distraught, but figured it was due to the stress of studying for some exam. He soon learned different.

When the university psychiatrist disclosed to the media that Whitman had discussed the tower fantasy, he was criticized for not foreseeing that Whitman might act out, especially since he had noticed Whitman's level of hostility. Criminologists said it was a cry for help, but it's quite difficult to predict who will carry out such threats—especially at the time, when mass murders were so rare.

Whitman's actions inspired a 15-year-old boy to shoot the town marshal in Sweetwater, Texas, the following day. After listening to news accounts, the boy said that he could not stop himself. And he was not the only one to see a strategy for himself in what Whitman had done. Whitman's act would reverberate through successive decades.

MASS MURDER AND BRAIN SCIENCE

Mass killers like Whitman have a plan. They want to get even. They tend to be mostly white males in their 30s who feel that life is becoming overwhelming. They blame others for their failures and see no way out. They're irate, even enraged, and they can't let go of that. Often they're angry at society, so their targets are random representations. Sometimes they have pushed themselves so much that they feel they can't reach goals that they themselves have set. They view themselves as failures and can't take it anymore. But they blame others for this.

Often their act is a suicide mission. They go kill and then expect to be killed in the process. Their life is too painful to go on. Despite Whitman's escape plan, it seemed more likely from the position into which he placed himself that day that he believed he would die. Yet it also seems clear from his stock of provisions that he thought he'd last longer than he did.

The incident seemed to be linked to events that had enraged him, but after Whitman's death, at his autopsy, it was found that he had a glioblastoma multiforme, a walnut-size (some accounts say pecan-size) malignant brain tumor situated near the amygdala (some say over the brain stem). Some people thought this condition had a causal influence on Whitman's violence. A panel of doctors admitted the tumor could have caused pressure and headaches. No one could say whether the amphetamines might have had a complicating effect.

The debates over this began. Whitman's friends thought the shooting had been uncharacteristic of him, but those experts who had studied violence at that time believed that the degree of preplanning evident from Whitman's writings eliminated the possibility that the incident had resulted from a brain abnormality. To be caused by a brain disorder, they insisted, the violence would have to have been spontaneous and unconnected to Whitman's life events. In *Mass Murder*, Jack Levin and James Fox state that "Whitman had written his detailed plan for mass killing in his diary days before the actual massacre, describing not only how he planned to protect his position on the tower and how he planned to escape, but even what he was going to wear. Moreover, Whitman's killing spree did not occur in quick succession."[1] They thereby dismiss it as being episodic, spontaneous violence.

Whitman's long-standing anger at his father and several recent setbacks seemed sufficient reason for saying that he just could not handle his frustration and so he had acted out. But that's a psychodynamic approach, and accepting it too quickly may be a failure to probe more deeply into the neurological possibilities. Upon reexamination of this theory, it's possible that pressure from the tumor had been gradual and that Whitman had felt uncomfortable, disorientated, and agitated as a result, but had been unable to explain it. In that case, he might have placed meaning on his physical deterioration, which over the course of time evolved into blame and frustration. Often those who feel vague unease try to figure out a reason for it. It's not inconsistent with the evaluation of organic diseases, especially one that affects the brain's emotional centers, for the affected person to develop a plan for acting out his or her increasingly tense emotionality. The more we learn about people with bipolar disorder and schizophrenia, for example, the more we find that such disorders have key organic components that influence an affected person's misperceptions of, and behavioral reactions to, the world around them. Recent research offers more insight.

In July 2000 a report was published in *Science* by Dr. Richard Davidson at the University of Wisconsin at Madison. Studies by him and his colleagues indicated that convicted murderers, those with aggressive or antisocial disorders, and other violence-prone people showed a distinct brain pattern on image scans. The researchers evaluated more than five hundred people and compared their brain scans to a group of people considered to be normal.

The findings showed a relationship among three brain regions that play a part in the control of negative emotions—the orbital frontal cortex, the anterior cingulate cortex, and the amygdala. The first area assists in restraining impulsive emotional outbursts, the second deals with responses to conflict, and the third, the amygdala, activates fear reactions. In the study, brain activity in violent people was diminished or absent in those areas that inhibit reactions when compared to the control groups, but the amygdala maintained normal or increased activity.

If this research bears fruit in the future, it could help to identify children at risk for future violence. But it could also unfairly label them, as well as miss environmental factors that might either enhance or diminish aggression, and this is an ethical dilemma that concerns the National Institute for Mental Health. Yet given recent research on the brain's plasticity, early treatment could be both beneficial and preventative.

We like to believe that our emotions can be controlled by our conscious, rational brain. However, our most primitive brain circuits are primed toward more volatile emotions, responding strongly to fear before reason. Joseph Ledoux, a neuroscientist at the Center for Neural Science at New York University, discovered a parallel pathway for information that goes straight to the emotional centers. In his 1996 books *The Emotional Brain,* he discusses how the amygdala seems to get activated when in a state of distress. The information is routed from the thalamus to the amygdala, which is part of the limbic system, the brain's emotional headquarters. The amygdala's job is to scan the information for danger, particularly with regard to what it "remembers" from previous dangerous situations.

If a certain situation once seemed dangerous, that same (or a similar) situation will trigger an alarm. The body will react without the person evaluating how rational or appropriate the reaction is. The amygdala sends out a distress signal to the entire brain, signaling physiological responses such as an increased heartbeat, sweat, and heightened blood pressure, to release hormones that prepare us for defense. We respond before we even consciously grasp what may be happening. The emotional brain blocks out the thinking brain, because the message gets to it faster and by the time the emotion of fear or anger—even rage—floods our thoughts, the reaction feels correct. The thinking brain is hijacked.

The amygdala is mature at birth. It gets busy at once processing emotion-laden situations before we have a chance to think about them. It then makes judgments based on past events that we may not even re-member in ways that we can process. It stores the raw material of the most primitive and basic emotional memories. Even crude similarities can spur eruptions. If your mother neglected you for long periods of time, you may act out against a spouse who walks away during a discussion. The memories trigger the reaction, not the situation itself.

The part of the brain that registers and stores factual information, the hippocampus, does not develop until around age 2, and under severe stress, such as child abuse, may even shrink and fail to operate as well as it should. In contrast, stress enhances the amygdala's functions.

In the September 2003 issue of *Scientific American*, which was devoted entirely to the latest brain research, an article on the brain's stress path-ways confirmed this. Stress pathways, a sidebar notes, are feedback loops in the brain that can amplify a reaction or response. A perceived threat activates the reasoning centers, which send a message to the amygdala for response mediation. Yet the amygdala may already be in motion from a preconscious signal that beats the reasoning centers. The amygdala releases cortico-tropin, a hormone that signals the brain stem to activate the nervous system. Simultaneously, epinephrine travels a different messenger route to stimulate the release of other hormones, which prepare the body to take action—fight or flight. Chronic, un-resolved stress may overproduce these hormones and keep activating the stress pathways.

Thus a "myg" attack, influenced by stress and a pattern of anger, could have been a factor in Whitman's violence. An inability to restrain the fear and anger in some parts of the brain could have allowed those emotions to explode. Whitman appeared to sense something wrong with his brain. He may have been correct. But the research, while progressing, cannot make such a diagnosis definitive.

Consider these findings in the debate over the next mass murderer, who may well have been influenced by Speck and Whitman, but who seemed to have developed a way of processing the world and setting his life's goals without any overtly stressful triggers—at least none that were clear in the aftermath.

BLACK AMBITION

On November 12, 1966, high school senior Robert Smith, 18, was obsessed with making a name for himself and had decided that murder was the way to do it. He had fantasies about stabbing women and had nearly ambushed his own father with a knife. A loner and a good student in Mesa, Arizona, he had learned what little there was to know about mass murder to that point—and only months before had just witnessed the media frenzy over both Whitman and Speck. Mass murder appealed to him for its rather sensational quality, and his parents had given him a .22-caliber pistol for his birthday—the same month that Charles Whitman had gone on his shooting spree.

Smith preset the number of victims he hoped to kill at forty. Then he looked around for potential targets and settled on a school not far from his home: the Rose-Mar College of Beauty. The incident was carefully planned. He prepared his equipment the night before, similar to Whitman's preparations, and the next morning he went to the college. He encountered five women in the shop, according to the *Arizona Republic*, along with a child and a baby. To show them he meant business, he fired a warning shot into a mirror. Then he ordered them to go into a back room and lie down with their heads together.

When one woman began to pray, this act so enraged Smith that he shot her in the head. Then he shot the others. One of them, Bonita Harris, pretended to be dead but actually survived to describe what happened. The baby, wounded, also survived, because her mother had shielded her. But four women and a 3-year-old child were dead. Smith later said that he also had to stab the child, because after he'd shot her she kept moving around. He said he shot the baby because she was going to grow into an adult one day.

The police quickly closed in and had him in custody by 9:30 that morning. Smith was found guilty and sentenced to death, but the federally mandated moratorium on the death penalty in 1972 that had affected all people around the country on death row commuted his multiple sentences to life.

Robert Smith's court-appointed psychiatrist diagnosed him as schizophrenic, but others thought him merely antisocial. He said he had felt exhilarated after the shootings and had no regrets. The idea that he felt like an all-powerful god and had no feelings for anyone else was a strange notion in those days and seemed delusional in the hallucinatory way. Indeed, some people with schizophrenia do talk like that, but psychopaths actually feel that way as well—without dementia. Little was known then about psychopaths, although Hervey Cleckley had published a groundbreaking study in 1941, *The Mask of Sanity*.

Up until that time, starting in the nineteenth century, psychopathy had been referred to by such labels as "moral insanity" and "constitutional psychopathic inferiority." Having encountered this distinct personality type during the course of his work, Cleckley came up with sixteen traits that, in constellation, formed a specific pattern of perspective and behavior that he believed was closer to psychosis than neurosis—but not really either. Among these traits were irresponsibility, deceptiveness, self-centeredness, shallowness, lack of empathy, and a penchant for committing more types of crimes than would other offenders. Manipulative and charming, these people were also more violent, more likely to recidivate, and less likely to benefit from treatment. They could remove themselves, psychologically, from the true horror of their crimes and thus commit them without remorse.

Cleckley wrote introductions to successive editions of his book, commenting on the psychiatric community's hesitation to address this population. Where clinical assessment and treatment were concerned, psychopaths appeared to be on a back burner. Cleckley perceived that, because the syndrome was difficult to spot from outward symptoms, and because it had historically been mixed with other neuroses, psychiatric terminology failed to offer a clear way to address such people.

Not until the 1980s would psychopathy become diagnosable with a formal assessment instrument, developed by Dr. Robert Hare in Canada and known as the Psychopathy Checklist (PCL). Now revised, the PCL-R is in use throughout the world for assessment and risk prediction. "Psychopathy is a personality disorder," Hare wrote in his 1993 book, *Without Conscience,* "defined by a distinctive cluster of behaviors and inferred personality traits, most of which society views as pejorative."[2]

In other publications, he pointed out that among the most devastating features of psychopathy are a callous disregard for the rights of others and a propensity for predatory and violent behaviors. Without remorse, psychopaths charm and exploit others for their own gain. They lack empathy, and they manipulate, lie, and con others without regard for anyone's feelings.

That description sounds plain enough, but over the decades the concept and definition of psychopathy have gone through many changes. Unfortunately, some of these shifts have been the product of evolving fashion in the professional community rather than an attempt to better identify the members of a specific population. While psychopathy was among the first personality disorders that psychiatry formally recognized, it wasn't easy to crystallize a workable concept for unambiguous behavioral analysis. Even today there is confusion.

In 1952 the word "psychopath" was officially replaced in psychiatric nomenclatures with "sociopathic personality," although "sociopathy" had been in use since the 1920s, and these labels were eventually used interchangeably by many professionals under the heading of "personality disorder." Then, with the second edition of the *Diagnostic and Statistical Manual of Mental Disorders (DSM-II)* in 1968, "sociopathic personality" yielded to "personality disorder, antisocial type."

Yet there were no measurable diagnostic criteria for the disorder on which professionals could agree, so researchers looked for ways to devise some. Hare and his colleagues emerged with the single best method, but not without a lot of work. In 1970, Hare had published *Psychopathy: Theory and Research,* which set forth some ideas that would guide much of the research on psychopaths over the next two decades. Throughout the early 1970s, many researchers used different classification systems to address psychopathy, such as categories based on the *Minnesota Multiphasic Personality Inventory* and the *California Psychological Inventory.* However, this approach yielded too many different instruments.

Hare's first published work on his twenty-two-item research scale, the PCL, appeared in 1980. That was the same year that the *DSM-III* came out. Then the field began to divide.

Dr. Lee Robins, an eminent sociologist, focused the antisocial diagnosis strictly on behavior. The list of ten items submitted to the *DSM* committee for consideration as diagnostic symptoms consisted primarily of behavioral violations of social norms. A person needed to manifest only a few to be diagnosed with antisocial personality disorder. Researchers working on a more narrowly defined notion of the psychopath, which also included psychological criteria, believed this *DSM* category would include more types of people than merely psychopaths. That made it operationally unworkable.

Yet with some adjustments, the behavioral criteria for an antisocial diagnosis were continued over the next two decades in the *DSM-III-R* and the *DSM-IV.* Accordingly, clinicians who use these manuals look for symptoms in people over 18 who are not otherwise psychotic, and who since age 15 have shown a pervasive pattern of disregard for, and violation of, the rights of others. Among these behaviors, the person shows evidence of at least three of the following:

- failure to conform to lawful social norms
- deceitfulness
- impulsivity or failure to plan ahead
- irritability and aggressiveness, as indicated by repeated physical fights or assaults
- reckless disregard for safety of self or others

- consistent irresponsibility, as indicated by repeated failure to sustain consistent work behavior or honor financial obligations
- lack of remorse, as indicated by being indifferent about having hurt, mistreated, or stolen from another

So while clinicians now had a list of explicit criteria, a diagnosis of antisocial personality disorder (APD) proved to be impractical for those who were researching psychopathy. While most psychopaths admittedly may fit the criteria for APD, many people diagnosed with APD are not psychopaths. In other words, there were now two different diagnostic instruments to assess two different populations that overlapped on many but not all of the listed criteria.

To simplify the idea and add a dimension not yet fully explored as such, Dr. Robert Rieber wrote, in *Psychopaths in Everyday Life*, that these people are prone to a profound dissociation that affects how they process language, how they behave, and how they form specific goals. He noted in Cleckley's book a reference to the idea that we all possess some degree of ability to not respond to the moral or social requirements of a situation, with the psychopath taking this to an everyday extreme. Rieber developed his understanding of the psychopath as an individual who pathologically breaks ranks with his conscience in a way over which he has no control. That makes him incapable of human concern and involvement except in the context of exploitation. Adaptive psychopaths, or those who live quietly within a private psychopathic fantasy, are able to fool others with a public persona until such time as they have a serious run-in with the law. That is, they can have long periods of seemingly normal behavior, although they are really quite abnormal. It's all just part of their game.

Rieber indicates that psychopaths can be distinguished according to four characteristics distilled from the work of others: thrill-seeking, pathological glibness, the antisocial pursuit of power, and the absence of guilt. They create situations of danger to feel alive, they experience no deterring emotions, and they dissociate from their behavior and its consequences as an alternative to becoming psychotic. In fact, says Rieber, their reliance on dissociation is a hallmark of the disorder. It's like the dissociated state that characterizes multiple personality disorder in that it's not controllable, but it manifests in a different kind of syndrome that relies on extreme narcissism and the quest for power as adaptive traits.

It seems likely, given what we now believe we know about psychopaths, that today Robert Smith would have been diagnosed with APD or psychopathy.

IN WHITMAN'S SHADOW

In San Ysidro, California, on July 18, 1984, at around 4 P.M., a local McDonald's was busy serving families. A man named James Oliver Huberty, 41, barged in armed with a semiautomatic rifle, an Uzi, and a semiautomatic pistol. He yelled to the patrons, "Everybody, get down on the floor or I'll kill somebody."[3]

Frightened and confused people attempted to comply, but the impatient Huberty started shooting anyway. He was there to take lives. Some of his victims tried to run, while others were simply approaching the building, unwittingly walking right into their deaths. After ten minutes of this shooting frenzy, many people lay dead and wounded, most of them teenagers or children. During the chaos, an employee in the kitchen managed to phone the police. Huberty remained there, shooting.

Officers arrived and called a SWAT team to take over. No one knew how many people inside were firing weapons, or whether hostages might be endangered if the team fired from outside, so they had to be careful. Huberty fired on them as they took position.

For another hour, he kept shooting, although at a slower pace. Then an employee of the restaurant managed to escape and was able to give the SWAT team some needed information about Huberty's position inside. The sharpshooters got ready. Several shot into the building but hit nothing, and then one bullet found its target, hitting Huberty in the chest and killing him.

His final victim tally was twenty dead and twenty wounded, one of whom would die later, making twenty-one dead. It was deemed the worst single-day incident of mass killing in the country's history—and once again an incident involving some man walking into the midst of strangers out of the blue to bring death and destruction.

Was he just angry or was he ill? It turned out that Huberty had suffered from depression, and possibly something worse. His wife, Etna, had tried to persuade him the day before to see a psychiatrist. She knew that he'd been hearing voices and believed that he might have been hallucinating. He'd been unemployed for several weeks and no matter how hard he tried he'd been unable to get on his feet. He had also lost a job the previous year in another state, which was the trigger that had brought him and his family to California.

Huberty had grown increasingly angry over his failure and Etna had grown fearful of what he might do, so as a last resort he called a local clinic. He was told that someone would soon get back to him. He waited, but that call never came, a broken promise in his mind just like so many others. It added one more dimension to his anger at society.

People who knew him who talked about him after the massacre had seen his hot temper and some described him as having "unfocused rage." He seemed perpetually disappointed in himself and in others. Some were not surprised by his actions. As they questioned people, the police retraced Huberty's steps.

On the morning of July 18, he went to traffic court to settle a violation and then met his wife and daughter at a McDonald's for lunch. Then they went together to the zoo in San Diego. All the while, he brooded about the fact that the clinic had never called. It was just one more indication that society in general was against him and would prevent him from getting ahead. He could not even get help from social agencies. So he said to his wife, "Society's had their chance."[4] She did not know what he meant.

The family returned to their apartment and Huberty said he was going out. He kissed his wife. She asked if he needed money and he told her no. He added something odd that she was later to remember with regret. Huberty said, "I'm going hunting—hunting humans."[5] He grabbed several guns from his impressive collection and went half a mile away to another McDonald's, where he started shooting.

A massacre such as this often occurs directly after a triggering event, such as the loss of a job or some significant failure. The perpetrators view themselves as going downhill fast. They can't perceive their own resources to bounce back, in part because they're paranoid and insecure, fearing that any effort they expend will get them nowhere, digging them in deeper.

In addition, Huberty may have been mentally ill. The more random a shooting is, with no familiar targets, the more likely it is that such a person may have psychotic delusions. That's something we will never know about James Huberty, but clues pointed to the possibility. Etna said that she thought he had been hallucinating, and he certainly showed behavior that frightened her.

When personnel at the clinic were later questioned about his call the day before, they claimed that he had sounded lucid and rational, not at all dangerous. They had concluded that it was not an emergency. Apparently, the notes on it were filed away. Etna had actually tried calling them to ask why they had not returned her husband's call, and they told her there was no record of his call. She suggested that he might be dangerous, so they advised her to call the police. She did not do so. She was likely at a loss to know just what to do. Turning her husband in to the police was quite a different proposition from getting him some professional help.

Another factor that emerges in Huberty's situation is that he had no real resources in the area. He'd left his support system behind when he moved to California the year before. With no one to turn to and with burdensome responsibilities weighing him down, the picture probably looked altogether bleak.

Mass murderers generally use weapons that allow them to kill from a distance. They also have developed a psychological distance, even with those they love. As they grow isolated and disillusioned, they look for someone to blame and punish, so their executions transform even loved ones into objects. Yet are they just angry and ready to wreak revenge, as many experts indicate, or have we seen evidence that severe mental illness makes its own contribution?

The next chapter offers cases that show how paranoia and hallucinations can undoubtedly be involved.

CHAPTER 4

Mental Illness and the Compulsive Killer

TALKING CRAZY

Like James Huberty, George Hennard chose a crowded restaurant for his attack, and like Huberty, the issue of mental illness was considered but not altogether resolved. These massacres had several things in common, and both remain somewhat unresolved.

Hennard had a habit of "talking crazy." He'd tell people who waited on him things such as, "I want you to tell everyone that if they don't quit messing around my house, something awful is going to happen."[1] Echoing Howard Unruh at times from more than forty years earlier, Hennard was upset about the recent hearings in which Anita Hill had accused judicial candidate Clarence Thomas of sexual harassment, and the idea that a woman would bring forth such charges greatly angered him. Women, he said, should know their place. Those who did not he called "female vipers."

Having just turned 35 on October 15, 1991, Hennard rammed his blue Ford pickup the following day at lunchtime through the plate glass window of Luby's Cafeteria in Killeen, Texas. He hit an elderly man, and the patrons who ran to the victim's aid initially believed that the whole thing was some freak accident. But then Hennard, who had seemed uncharacteristically calm to those he encountered that morning, jumped from the truck with a Glock 17 semiautomatic and a Ruger P89 and started to shoot. He aimed for the head or chest of every person he could see, shooting fast so that no one could escape. Yelling that it was "payback day," he snarled at people to "take that!"

He shot some of his victims more than once to make certain the wounded were dead. Stopping once to reload, he had enough clips full of ammunition to spray the weapon many times across the room. Inexplicably, he allowed one women with a child to leave, although she was forced to leave behind her dead mother. One person who escaped recalled later, "He was smiling, kind of a grin, like a smirk."[2]

The police arrived and shouted at Hennard to drop his weapon. He ignored them and continued to shoot at customers. They took aim at him and fired, so he turned his weapons on them. Two bullets hit him, forcing a retreat, and he took cover. Apparently he realized it was now over. In a flash, he put one of his pistols to his head and pulled the trigger. His last bullet took his final victim, himself. When police went in to look around, twenty-two people in the restaurant lay dead, with twenty-three wounded. No one could fathom a reason why anyone would do this.

While Hennard was a loner, he was not exactly a loser. He lived in a nice home and was fairly attractive. His father was a surgeon. He was not the typical angry man down on his luck. Yet he had made an appeal to be reinstated in the merchant marines, in which he had served for eight years. In February, six months before the shooting incident, his appeal had been denied. He had also long exhibited an extreme hatred of women, shouting at them in public. Someone who had served with him said he'd harbored a violent hatred toward his domineering mother. He thought of her as a snake, and had an unfounded delusion that women were harassing him.

Yet when he had purchased the guns used in the rampage, Hennard had been living with his mother in Nevada. He had given off signals of what was coming, mentioning to someone a month before the assault that he might kill someone. He had also tried unsuccessfully to sell his guns. In the end, he'd decided to use them to avenge some imagined insult and then end his own life. Although there is no record that he sought help or was assessed as mentally ill, his reputation for "talking crazy" and for lashing out without provocation, as well as his extreme beliefs about how women treated him, could be considered the red flags of a paranoia-induced psychosis.

Similarly, Thomas Hamilton obsessed about his reputation for some twenty years after he was dropped as a scoutmaster in the Scottish Highlands on suspicion of inappropriate behavior. He had become known to the boys in Dunblane as "Mr. Creepy," and it was rumored that he liked taking photographs of boys without their shirts. A week before he acted out, he wrote a letter to Queen Elizabeth II to complain about an imagined campaign calculated to ruin him.

On March 13, 1996, he armed himself with four weapons and went to the Dunblane primary school. Once there, he entered the gymnasium. Students, ages 5 and 6, were sitting in circles for a class, and Hamilton started shooting at them. He killed thirteen students and a teacher, while wounding fifteen students and another teacher before shooting himself in their midst. Three of the wounded kids died later, making Hamilton's death toll for the day, including himself, eighteen.

In the British "public enquiry," it was noted that Hamilton appeared to have a persecution complex and delusions of grandeur. He also hated fat children and blamed parents for their state. When he opened a series of boys' clubs after his scouting career failed, the numbers of enrollees diminished due to his militaristic style, and it was noted that he apparently liked dominating young boys. In the papers, comments from a psychologist and psychiatrist about his character during the six months leading up to the massacre included the following observations:

1. He was abusive toward parents who withdrew their sons from his club.
2. He was deceptive.
3. He did not allow others to question how he ran his clubs.
4. He had written numerous letters to the Scouts and the police regarding his dismissal.
5. He felt victimized.
6. He was highly sensitive to what people thought of him.
7. He tried to keep the boys from having contact with their parents.
8. He had no close relationships with adults.
9. He had a strong interest in firearms and had recently purchased the firearms he used in the shooting incident; others observed that he treated his guns as if they were his children.

In short, Hamilton became more desperate as his clubs failed and, with no support system, found some consolation in his shooting activities, which probably gave him the idea that he could do something about his feelings of persecution and fear of what others were saying.

DIAGNOSIS

Psychotic disorders are a cluster of severe mental disorders characterized by specific symptoms, such as impairment of the abilities to think coherently, respond appropriately, comprehend reality as others know it, behave appropriately, and make oneself understood. Several different conditions can result in a display of psychotic symptoms, such as severe depression, bipolar disorder, schizophrenia, some forms of borderline personality disorder, and some examples of substance abuse. A person with psychotic symptoms such as fixed delusions and hallucinations cannot function well in daily life. They may adopt a suspicious and hostile manner. Delusions of paranoia or grandiosity may trigger acting out against others, especially when coupled with auditory command hallucinations to do so. In many cases, they have a religious context.

Both severe depression and schizophrenia have played a role in mass murder. Those who feel persecuted and cannot diminish the burden with medication, or support may allow the fear and anger to build into fantasies of revenge until some incident or ideation finally pushes them into action.

Writing in the 1970s, psychiatrist Donald T. Lunde made the statement in *Murder and Madness* that mass murderers either have paranoid schizophrenia or are sexual sadists. By that he categorized the mass murderer, as defined in this book, as legally insane, while the sexual sadists were serial killers. He had not yet been exposed to workplace violence, school rampages, or even the visionary mass murders, aside from those of Charles Manson's gang. It was easier for him to make such diagnoses because so few cases were known at the time he was writing.

As Dr. Richard Noll points out in *The Encyclopedia of Schizophrenia and the Psychotic Disorders,* the concept of schizophrenia has changed over time, with various causal attributions, from viruses to bad mothering to brain impairment. The term was coined in a 1908 publication by Swiss psychiatrist Eugen Bleuler for a group of psychotic disorders that appeared to have dissociated psychological functions. He thought the illness was characterized by "a specific type of alteration" in thinking, feeling, and relating to the external world.

A good example is seen in Colin Ferguson, because after his episode of mass murder, he defended himself in court, exhibiting his illness to the world. He also stands apart from many other mass murderers in that he was black. He's not alone in this regard, but he's rare. His case was documented in the *New York Times* and on a documentary for the A&E Network.

On December 7, 1993, a late afternoon commuter train left Manhattan for Long Island. It was packed with people trying to get home. Colin Ferguson, 34, boarded at the Jamaica-Queens station, armed with a 9-mm handgun and a bag of bullets. He was angry. He'd spent most of the day letting his anger fester.

On the train he took a seat and watched others get on board. As the train started up, commuters closed their eyes or tried to read books or newspapers. They were thinking about dinner and seeing their families.

Ferguson suddenly stood and fired his gun at a woman. He continued to shoot, hitting passengers in the third car of the train. Some tried to get into the next car or hide behind seats. Those who saw the shooter reported later that he had a blank look on his face.

He fired fifteen rounds in approximately ten seconds, and then re-loaded, walking up the aisle and shooting. When he stopped, someone shouted to others to grab him. Three people did so, and he pleaded not to be hurt. At the next stop, he was removed. In less than two minutes, nineteen people had been wounded and six were dead.

Ferguson was arrested and taken to police headquarters. They found two torn notes in his pocket giving scribbled reasons for what he had done. "Nassau County is the Venue," said one, and "New York City was spared because of my respect for Mayor David Dinkins" said the other.[3] He also referred to "racist Caucasians." Under questioning, he asked about his victim count. He denied nothing, and justified his actions by claiming that he had been persecuted his entire life by prejudice.

His lawyers hoped to use "black rage" for an insanity defense, but Ferguson decided to dispense with them altogether. He had come to America from Jamaica at the age of 24 to further his education, but he'd encountered what he defined as a "huge conspiracy" against him. Sup-posedly, everyone was trying to hold him back from doing something important. He had been disruptive enough at two colleges to be asked to leave, and his marriage had lasted only two years. At the time of the shootings, he was unemployed, broke, and living alone in a one-room apartment. He had tried to get more money from workmen's compen-sation for an injury suffered on the job, but this had been denied to him on the very day that he decided to board the commuter train and start shooting.

Ferguson did not want to see a psychiatrist or have his records reviewed, so he rejected an insanity defense. All he had to do to pass the compe-tency test was describe the role of the prosecutor—and he was led along by the judge. He then offered his defense theory: He had not shot the pas-sengers on the train. He said that a police officer had told him that some-one else was actually responsible and that he was being set up.

His lawyers insisted this was proof of his incompetency, but he con-tinued to refuse to accept psychiatric assessment or care. Two attorneys with a mission, Ron Kuby and William Kuntsler, got involved to try to get him to change his mind, but he would not. He was judged compe-tent to stand trial. In October, to get attorneys off his back, Ferguson decided to defend himself.

The standards for competence to defend oneself in American courts are low. There are several types of legal competencies, from competency to waive one's Miranda rights to competency to stand trial. There's even competency to be executed. The legal doctrine of competence originated in English common law, at a time centuries ago when defendants had to argue their own cases. People are declared competent when they have voluntarily waived their rights and they currently have no mental disease or defect prohibiting them from understanding the proceedings, the parties involved, and the consequences. In the twentieth century, the U.S. Supreme Court considered various competency issues and held that competency should be presumed and incompetence proven with a preponderance of the evidence.

Being judged competent is about having a "good understanding." It does not imply normal mental functioning. Unabomber Ted Kaczynski, diagnosed as having paranoid schizophrenia, was declared competent (which became a moot point when he pleaded guilty).

Ferguson's legal advisers, Kuby and Kuntsler, continued to try to prove him psychotic. They got a defense psychiatrist to testify that Ferguson was incompetent. Yet the prosecutor said that Ferguson was merely malingering to throw things off track: He was scheming and manipulative, and should be judged competent.

The judge once more found him competent—Ferguson knew the dangers of representing himself and had the right to do so. Ferguson assured the judge he would be a formidable opponent to the prosecution team.

On January 26, 1996, the case went to trial. The district attorney had fifty people who could identify Ferguson as the shooter on the train. In addition, the gun proven to have been used in the shootings belonged to him. Ferguson's job was to convince the jury he was not the man. In his opening statement, he said that the only reason there were ninety-three counts on the indictment was that it matched the year 1993—the year of the incident. "Had it been 1925," he insisted, "it would have been 25 counts."[4] He claimed that he was being stereotyped and victimized by a conspiracy to destroy him. The person who had committed the crime was a white gunman who had taken his weapon from the bag while he was asleep.

One eyewitness after another identified Ferguson as the shooter. Many of them had been shot by him. One man who had tackled him was accused by Ferguson to be the real killer, because he'd grabbed the gun. Since President Bill Clinton had honored the men who had grabbed him, Ferguson wanted to subpoena the president. He also suggested that everyone who had testified against him had been influenced by pretrial publicity.

When the time came to present his own case, he insisted that no one's identification of him was credible. Then he said he needed more time.

He could not get his witnesses to testify. He said that certain handwriting and ballistics experts were in fear of their lives. He did call a homicide detective in a failed effort to prove that some other Colin Ferguson was the killer.

Then a witness came forward to testify for the defense. Raul Diaz said that he was on the train and had seen an Asian man press a computer chip into Ferguson's head to activate him to commit the crime. The Asian had told Diaz to witness what he was doing as he pressed a remote control. Ferguson apparently declined to call this witness. He rested his case and spoke for three hours to sway the jurors to his side. He insisted there was reasonable doubt and he begged the jurors to see him as a persecuted human being. Instead, they found Colin Ferguson guilty on all counts. He exhibited no reaction. In March 1996, Ferguson was sentenced to six consecutive life terms.

Legal experts and psychologists debated whether Ferguson should ever have been allowed to represent himself. The district attorney said Ferguson had schooled himself in the law and fought for his innocence, so he was not in the "other world" that some mental health experts insisted he was in. Yet his opening statement, his delusions of persecution, his idea that he was being framed for someone else's crime, and his attempt to accuse another Colin Ferguson all indicate dissociation from reality. Without a full-scale assessment, both sides could only guess at Ferguson's true condition.

A more telling case was that of a woman who went on a rampage in 1985.

NOT JUST LONE WHITE MALES

Mass killers are not always white and not always male. Criminologists tend to claim that mass killers are not "crazy" or insane, but this approach is too simplistic to account for all the cases. It's easy to speak in stereotypes, but that offers little understanding about the incidents that occur or the people who perpetrate them.

While most female mass killers tend to turn their madness or rage on those closest to them—their children—one proved quite close in spirit to her male counterparts, even in the way she dressed. Her story was covered in the *Philadelphia Inquirer,* and as unusual as she is among mass murderers, few criminologists speaking on the topic even acknowledge her. Yet her case is a lesson against quick pronouncements.

On October 30, 1985, midafternoon shoppers at the Springfield Mall outside Philadelphia, Pennsylvania, were startled by gunfire. Outside in the parking lot, someone was shooting. But when a woman entered, carrying a semiautomatic rifle and dressed in olive-green military fatigues, a knit cap, and black boots, many of them believed it was just some Halloween prank. They were wrong.

Near a restaurant's entrance, a child, age 2, lay dead, and two children were wounded. Outside, a number of people had run for cover, just barely eluding the shooter's bullets. The 20-something, medium-sized woman aimed directly at shoppers who failed to move fast enough and shot randomly inside several stores. One person, a 67-year-old man, was hit three times.

No one stopped the woman as she made her way, muttering to herself, through the pedestrian area. Several people fell to the floor, some of them bleeding badly. A woman yelled, "Help my husband, help my husband!" The shooting seemed to go on and on, although it lasted only four minutes, ending when John Laufer, a graduate student, braved the tirade and grabbed the shooter. "I'm a woman," she said, "and I have family problems and I have seizures."[5]

Laufer sat her down in a chair in a shoe store and told her to remain there. He then returned with a security guard, who placed the shooter under arrest. Laufer later said he thought the woman had been firing blanks as a prank. Just before he had stopped her, she had raised the rifle directly at him.

The toll that day was two dead and eight wounded. One of the wounded, a 69-year-old man, would later die, bringing the total deaths from this rampage to three. Those who worked at the mall knew this woman. Her name was Sylvia Seegrist and she frequented the place, often harassing customers. By the next day, it was learned that Seegrist had been trying to get a prescription filled at the mall drugstore earlier for tranquilizers, but the pharmacist had refused to do it because she did not have her Welfare card.

At her arraignment, which she attended barefoot, she indicated that she had expected to die. Asked her phone number, she rattled off a long string of random numbers in a voice charged with anger. She also lashed out with the statement that she wished she had never been born, and told the court that the reason for her rampage was trouble with her parents. Finally she said, "Do you have a black box? That is my testimony."[6]

There was no doubt that Sylvia Seegrist had a long record of mental illness. She had been diagnosed at the age of 15 as a person with a mental disorder so serious that she faced a lifetime of drugs or hospitalization, or both. Since her illness involved a developing hostility and aggression, she quickly alienated family and friends. That left her lonely as well as disoriented, with no one to help her find her bearings. She was hospitalized a dozen times and then given drugs. No professional followed her case, although she saw several different psychiatrists for the medication.

Since she often did not take the drugs appropriately or they did not work well, her delusions and anger worsened. In the weeks prior to the shooting, people who knew her said that she had been acting "terribly psychotic." Her mother, Ruth Seegrist, told reporters that Sylvia was "completely out of touch with reality."[7] She had urged her daughter to commit herself earlier that week, but Seegrist had responded that she'd rather go to prison. Trying to enlist in the army, she had been discharged from boot camp over her problems.

People in the area were long familiar with her as an eccentric character. She often dressed in army fatigues and went in and out of the stores, harassing customers. She also showed up in a local health club, fully dressed in her fatigues to work out, and she could be found in a library muttering to herself. She was obsessed with the idea of "negative energy." At one point during the year before, she had attempted to strangle her mother. Her psychiatrist at the time had objected to the court releasing her from commitment, but he was ignored.

In retrospect, people were amazed that she managed to acquire a Ruger semiautomatic .22-caliber rifle in her dangerous state of mind, but she did. She had tried getting it at K-Mart, but store employees had sensed something wrong and lied to her about not having one in stock. A week later, she went to the sporting goods counter at Best Products and after saying on a form that she did not have a history of mental illness (which they were not required to check), she got her gun. Her illness had a decade to fester until she decided to act out.

Before the massacre that day, Seegrist had gone to the mall and left. She worked out for half an hour, speaking to no one. She went to the library but did not stay. Then she showed up back at the mall. Removing the .22 semiautomatic rifle from the trunk of her car, she started shooting before she even set foot inside.

Over the next year after the rampage, Seegrist underwent extensive psychiatric examinations, although she was found to be competent to stand trial, which began seven months after the shooting. She was found guilty but mentally ill and given three consecutive life sentences, with a minimum of ten years each. Sent to a psychiatric facility for evaluation, she was eventually moved to the state correctional institution at Muncy. The inept way that her case had been handled influenced a major overhaul of Pennsylvania's mental heath system.

Only two and a half years after Seegrist's massacre, as Seegrist was being moved to a prison, another woman meticulously planned a mass murder that still defies comprehension. She succeeded in killing only one person, but she intended the toll to be much higher. And she was not the only woman with this kind of lethal intent.

Laurie Wasserman Dann, too, did not achieve a high victim count in terms of actual deaths, but her aim to kill was clearly that of a mass murderer. On May 20, 1988, in Illinois, she shot six children, poisoned six other people, and shot one adult before committing suicide. She also tried to bomb an elementary school and set fire to a nursery school. Only a young boy actually died from the shooting incident, while the others were wounded or made quite ill. Beforehand, Dann had assembled a list of the names of many of her intended victims, and to them she had delivered packages of arsenic-laced food. She left no explanation for her actions, but her acquaintances indicated that she had a history of anger and mental problems. Yet she had never been hospitalized or diagnosed, so her case remains a mystery.

Both of these women were acting under the pressure of some delusion and both demonstrated behavior more typical of male mass murderers, except for Dann's use of poison. They both apparently suffered from a mental illness.

Then there was a team of killers who appear to have been spurred by the mental illness of one of them. Willie Steelman was 28 and Doug Gretzler 22. Steelman had once been committed to a mental institution, and when he met Gretzler, they started to kill and did not stop until they were caught. On October 28, 1973, they entered a house trailer in Mesa, Arizona, and shot to death the adolescent couple who lived there. They killed six more people in succession before they ended their spree with a massacre of nine people on November 6. Two days later, the killers were apprehended at a motel. Gretzler described their crimes in detail. Convicted in trials in two states, Steelman died in prison while Gretzler was executed in Arizona in 1998.

In another bizarre case, the mentally unstable killer fought hard to convince a jury he was faking his illness. Given the public anxiety of those times, he did not have to work hard at it.

PRETENDING TO BE SANE PRETENDING TO BE INSANE

In August 1969, Los Angeles, California, was shaken by a horrific murder spree that made international headlines. It appeared that several diabolical people had entered the home of Hollywood producer Roman Polanski and slaughtered five people in some ritual, including pregnant actress Sharon Tate. One of the killers used blood to write the word "pig" on a door. This gang left similar messages a day later at the home of

Leno and Rosemary LaBianca. Then a woman named Susan Atkins spilled the beans by bragging about it and the killers were arrested. The nation learned that a strange-looking drifter, Charles Manson, had gathered a "family" of homeless hippies from San Francisco's Haight-Ashbury neighborhood and ordered several of them to begin his murderous "revolution" against the white establishment. They had mindlessly obeyed and showed no remorse. This massacre will be addressed in Chapter 9 in detail, but here it provides context for another event that it inspired.

Six months later in North Carolina, on February 17, 1970, Green Beret Jeffrey MacDonald was found unconscious in his home, with his wife and two daughters stabbed and bludgeoned to death. He claimed that a group of hippies high on acid had attacked them all. What made his story suspicious was the fact that he had called for help, but that when military police responded, they found his home dark. Also, in the living room, where a table had been overturned, a magazine was opened to the story of the Manson murders. It appeared that MacDonald may have been inspired by that random attack to dispense with his family and throw the blame on rampaging drug-heads. He was initially charged, but those charges were dropped due to a mismanaged investigation, and later that year there was still talk of a blond woman in a floppy hat saying "groovy" as her male companions committed murder and mayhem. It would be a few years before MacDonald was again brought to trial and convicted, but before that occurred, it looked as if violent hippies were acting out around the country.

Back in California, where the Manson trial was in the news, another such massacre occurred not far away to the north, near Santa Cruz. On the evening of October 19, 1970, patrol officers spotted smoke in the Soquel hills. Responders arrived at 999 Rodeo Gulch Road, where a fire was racing through the mansion of eye surgeon Victor M. Ohta. They put out the fire, which clearly had been intentionally started, and looked around for possible victims. No one appeared to be there, so the fire chief went outside to the pool area to look for the fire hydrant that had been installed there. His flashlight caught something in the water, and on closer inspection, he could see someone floating. Calling for help, he retrieved a young boy. Then he stepped closer and saw that in the water's depths there were more shapes that appeared to be bodies. This crime scene was no mere arson.

According to reports the next day in the *Santa Cruz Sentinel*, the police had located five bodies. All of the victims were bound and blindfolded with colorful silk scarves. They were quickly identified by those acquainted with them. Among the dead were homeowner Victor Ohta, 46; his wife, Virginia, 43; his two sons, Derrick, 12, and Taggert, 11; and his secretary, Dorothy Cadwallader, 38. Each person had been shot from behind with a small-caliber gun.

Hoping they did not have a Tate-LaBianca type of assault here, the police searched for scrawled messages and told reporters they had found nothing of the kind, but Virginia Ohta's dark green 1968 Oldsmobile station wagon was missing.

"The grisly murder of five people has set a fuse burning on long smoldering tensions in this Oceanside city."[8] That was the sentiment of the Santa Cruz community published in the *Sentinel* soon after the discovery of the massacre.

Whoever the killers were, they appeared not to be motivated by robbery, so it seemed to many residents that the incident could only have been inspired by the same mindless urge to kill that had triggered Manson's followers. In fact, some people told reporters that Ohta had been bothered by hippies dropping into his secluded home. At one time, someone said, Dr. Ohta had chased six such vagabonds off his porch.

Then Virginia Ohta's car turned up. A slow-moving switch engine had smashed into it near Henry Cowell State Park. Whoever had stolen it had driven it about 150 feet into the tunnel, set fire to the seats, and then fled. A search of the area turned up nothing.

Not long afterward the media learned that a typewritten note had been found on the night of the murders. Its contents reinforced the fear that this was yet another "hippie" attack:

Halloween . . . 1970
    today world war 3 will begin as brought to you by the people of the free universe. From this day forward any one and ?/or company of persons who misuses the natural environment or destroys same will suffer the penalty of death by the people of the free universe.
    I and my comrades from this day forth will fight until death or freedom, against anything or anyone who does not support natural life on this planet, materialisum must die or man-kind will.
KNIGHT OF WANDS
KNIGHT OF CUPS
KNIGHT OF PENTICLES
KNIGHT OF SWORDS[9]

Then three men came forward with information and an arrest was made: John Linley Frazier, 24, also known as John Linley Pascal, who lived in a shack downhill from the Ohta property. His mother, Pat Pascal, a rabbit breeder, owned the property and rented out some of the dilapidated buildings there to college students and hippies. Frazier was a vegetarian who collected guns and did drugs, and whose personality seemed to have changed in recent weeks.

Frazier was arraigned on October 25, 1970, on five counts of murder. He stood with his hands tightly jammed into his denim coveralls, clearly agitated. On Frazier's behalf, Deputy Public Defender James Jackson entered a plea of not guilty and made arrangements for a psychiatric assessment.

The police gathered physical evidence that indicated that Frazier had indeed been inside the Ohta home. While people did not believe he could have killed five people by himself, retracing the victims' steps indicated that they had arrived at the house at different times. A close friend of Frazier's told reporters that he had been a reliable auto mechanic and a family man with a wife and 5-year-old child, but that he'd lately adopted a hippie lifestyle and sometimes talked in ways that made no sense. "All of a sudden he seemed like just another wired-up hippie."[10] He wore a strange symbol around his neck on a chain and often went without shoes and even without a last name. He wanted to be left alone.

Frazier's estranged wife, Dolores, offered information to police about his movements during the days prior to the crime. She had helped him clean out his shack on Saturday night and he had spent that night with her, leaving on Sunday afternoon with a loaded pistol, a pair of binoculars, and an orange backpack loaded with supplies. He'd left behind his driver's license and a book on his favorite subject, the Tarot cards, saying he would not need them any longer. Dolores also told authorities that the stolen green car had been left in an area where Frazier often went to swim and hike.

Yet even though the authorities were sure they finally had their man, they were nevertheless puzzled as to why Frazier would have acted as he had. From reports offered by his acquaintances, he clearly had planned the murders and had targeted October 19 as the date when "big things would be happening."

In the meantime, mental health experts were already at work. On October 26, one week after the murders, Frazier's court-appointed attorney, James Jackson, announced that Frazier was not sane, and that his act may have come as the result of head injuries he had received in an auto accident six months earlier. Jackson had been in contact with a psychologist, Dr. David Marlowe, for the purpose of assessment, and Marlowe had seen Frazier on four separate occasions. He reported that Frazier did not think or act normally.

On January 9 in jail, Frazier slashed his arm with a razor and was taken to a hospital for stitches. Ten days later, Jackson announced that he would modify Frazier's plea from innocent to innocent by reason of insanity. The judge appointed two psychiatrists to provide a sanity assessment for the court.

During the last days of November 1971, the jury convicted Frazier of the five murders. Then came the phase in which Frazier's sanity was the issue. Dr. David Marlowe offered testimony for the defense. He had spoken with Frazier thirty-five to forty times over the past year, and had heard three different version of what Frazier claimed he was doing on October 19. In late November 1970, Frazier apparently told Marlowe how the murders had been done. It was all right to state this in court, since the defense team was attempting to show that Frazier had been psychotic at the time of the offense.

Apparently, "voices from God" had commanded him to "seek vengeance on those who rape the environment." That afternoon, he went to the Ohta residence and found only Virginia Ohta at home. He had a .38 revolver, which he pointed at her as he used scarves that he found in the home to tie her hands together at the wrists. He told her she was evil. As Mrs. Ohta remained bound, Frazier waited for the rest of the family to return. He was upset to see animal skins inside the home—a violation of nature. He planned to kill each person who arrived, and he did so.

Frazier took them outside to the edge of the pool (or he took Ohta outside and then later brought the others), where he said he lectured Ohta about materialism and how it had a negative effect on the environment. He accused Ohta of ruining the Santa Cruz Mountains. He reported that Ohta then began to try to bribe him with material goods. Annoyed, Frazier suggested they burn down the house with everything inside. Ohta began to argue, so to shut him up, Frazier shoved him into the pool. As the man tried to get out, Frazier shot him three times.

He asked each of the others if they believed in God and they said yes, so he told them they had nothing to be afraid of. He walked behind each of his helpless victims and shot them at the base of the neck, killing the two women first, and then the two boys. He pushed them all into the pool. Then he went into the house to type the note that he left on Ohta's car. Afterward, he went about setting fires around the mansion.

Marlowe ended his account by saying that Frazier's stories were mostly disjointed and that he was insane and dangerous. He had gross disturbances in his thoughts and feelings. He also had visual and auditory hallucinations, with excessive religiosity, as seen by his underlining of passages in a Bible he carried. Frazier considered himself John from the Bible, to whom the Book of Revelation was addressed, and Frazier had developed a complex system of beliefs based in occultic number systems, astrology, reincarnation, and themes of immortality.

Donald T. Lunde was one of three forensic psychiatrists who testified, and he wrote about his experience in his book *Murder and Madness*. He contended that Frazier had paranoid schizophrenia and at the time of the murders was incapable of knowing that what he was doing was wrong. Frazier had told Lunde that he was a special agent sent from God to save the earth. Frazier's wife had heard these delusions as well during the summers of 1969 and 1970. Apparently he had grown increasingly more paranoid until he finally broke away from her and their child to go live in the woods. He trusted no one. Under Frazier's delusional system, Lunde said, the killing of certain people was necessary and thus not wrong. "He's crazy," Lunde had stated in court. He then amended that to, "He is unable to appreciate society's standards."[11]

On December 3, Frazier arrived with half of his head and face shaved, including one eyebrow. Marlowe explained that Frazier did this so the jury would think he was faking insanity and would find him sane and send him to the gas chamber. Frazier did not want to end up at a "fascist head factory." Marlowe said this was another indication of his distorted thinking.

District attorney Peter Chang had his own expert testify as well, psychiatrist John Peschau, who had interviewed Frazier for two hours. During the second week of December, Peschau, from Agnews State Hospital, said that Frazier suffered from a personality disorder, not psychosis. He was a sociopath, not schizophrenic, and he did appreciate what he had done and that it was wrong. Thus he was not legally insane. Not only that, but he would not learn from what he had done and was therefore a danger to society.

On December 16, Frazier showed up completely bald—no eyebrows, hair, mustache, or beard. This was clearly calculated for effect. Then as the judge instructed the jury, he sat reading George Orwell's novel *1984*. Earlier he had been reading a book on mental disorders.

Ultimately, the jury found Frazier guilty and sentenced him to death. However, when the Supreme Court declared capital punishment unconstitutional, Frazier's sentence was commuted to life in prison at San Quentin, where he remains as of this writing.

Providing a sense of his background, Dr. Lunde wrote that Frazier's parents had separated when he was 2 years old. When he was 5, his mother placed him in foster care. He ran away, was arrested for theft, and ended up in a series of juvenile detention facilities. He had a history of bedwetting, sleepwalking, and terrible nightmares. Eventually he was reunited with his mother, got married, and worked at a steady job. It seemed that he had made something of his life after all, but then things went downhill.

After his automobile accident in 1970, he told his wife that he'd received a message from God to stop driving. Then he decided he had been reincarnated with a mission to save the earth from materialism and to interpret the Book of Revelations for the rest of humanity. He believed the end of the world was at hand and there would be a revolution. To him, the Ohta home, which he could see from the small shack on his mother's property where he lived, represented all that was evil. It had to be destroyed and its occupants murdered. That was the only way to restore the natural beauty of the hillside.

While the juvenile facility records make no indication that Frazier had needed treatment, Lunde points out that the symptoms of schizophrenia often set in during the late teens or early adulthood. Frazier's evolving obsessions and attempts to convert people into disciples were consistent with this. On the day he left his wife to go to the Ohta estate, he talked about the approaching revolution and the need for some materialists to die. Lunde indicates that it's typical for paranoid schizophrenics to adopt current controversial issues as part of their delusional system. Dolores had tried over the past few months, without success, to get Frazier into treatment, so she had watched helplessly once again as he left on his "mission."

Despite the jury's verdict, Lunde insists that the case of John Linley Frazier presents a clear example of a murder committed within a state of psychosis. Had people not been so frightened about Mansonesque cults during that time, it's possible that they might have been able to better appreciate the influence on Frazier of his untreated mental illness and his head injury.

Despite the differing opinions, no one suggested a middle ground—"schizotaxia," coined in 1962 and the precursor to today's schizotypal personality disorder. People with this character disorder show a pervasive pattern of peculiar ideas, appearance, and behavior, and are uncomfortable in social situations. They may engage in magical thinking, talk to themselves, speak in an eccentric manner that makes no sense to others, show an unkempt appearance, and be suspicious or paranoid. This description seems consistent with what acquaintances said about Frazier, and since he did not complain of hallucinations, it might have been more accurate. However, since this is not full-blown schizophrenia, it would not have gotten him declared insane.

The situation is similar even today. Peter Odighizuwa, 45, was diagnosed with paranoid schizophrenia but found competent to stand trial for his killing of the Appalachian Law School's dean, a professor, and a student in 2002. Having flunked out, he came back to campus with a gun, killing three and wounding three. He pleaded guilty in exchange for six life sentences.

Mental illness issues are now commonplace discussions in crimes of this magnitude. They've also become a staple for assessments in one of the more recent developments in mass murders: the rash of shootings in the 1980s and 1990s by kids against classmates, teachers, families, and even strangers.

CHAPTER 5

Deadly Children

JUST FOR FUN

The Wat Promkunaram Buddhist temple stands at Cotton Lane and Maryland Avenue, west of Phoenix, Arizona. There, according to articles in the *Arizona Republic*, a worker bringing food on April 10, 1991, stumbled into a horrifying scene. In the small living room, next to a worn couch, all nine residents of the temple lay facedown and still in their orange-yellow saffron robes, positioned like the spokes in a wheel. The carpet around them was soaked in blood. When the police arrived, they found that the victims had been executed with bullets to the back of the head—eight males (six of them monks) and an elderly nun.

The Maricopa County sheriff's office called in the FBI. Former FBI profiler Gregg McCrary describes his involvement in *The Unknown Darkness*. Looking for evidence, investigators spotted an ash-filled ashtray in the middle of the circle of death, two fire extinguishers that had been sprayed randomly around the home, a pile of keys left on the kitchen table, and the word "Bloods" carved crudely into one wall. On the floor around the bodies were shell casings from a 20-guage shotgun and a .22-caliber weapon.

Within hours, the FBI profilers arrived. They had little behavioral evidence to go on, but some things stood out. For example, this had not been the work of professional hit men. To some extent it looked haphazardly staged, amateurish, and disorganized. The reference to "Bloods" seemed to be the way gangs such as Charles Manson's cutthroat group in 1969 "signed" their crimes, but it could have been an attempt to lay blame on an area gang. Two guns were used, indicating at least two perpetrators.

The evidence of two offenders who had engaged in random vandalism pointed to youth. They had used guns and ammunition that appeared to be from a basic hunting collection. It was an incomplete robbery—obviously valuable objects in the temple had been left intact—with violence undertaken most likely to eliminate witnesses. The ashes in the ashtray indicated that the incident had been extended over a period of time, perhaps for entertainment.

The police began to collect licensed guns of the right caliber for testing, to at least eliminate them as the murder weapon. They also went to pawn shops to see if anything stolen from the temple had been sold. All of the victims had lived there at the temple in a room with a single mattress and few possessions. In short, nothing in the victims' backgrounds appeared to have elevated their risk, individually or collectively, for becoming victims of violence.

On September 10, the Office of Special Investigations at Luke Air Force Base reported that base police had come across a .22-caliber rifle similar to the weapon suspected to have been used in the slayings. This weapon had initially been spotted on August 20 during a traffic stop, but since base police had not been informed, they had not realized its significance. At that time, the rifle had been on the passenger side of a vehicle driven by Rolando Caratachea, who was 17. Behind him in another car was Jonathan Doody, also 17, who was of Thai descent, and they'd been stopped for suspicious activity. The next day, the police again had stopped the boys, only this time they were in the same car. The police confiscated the rifle. But they then returned it. When the task force investigators learned about it, they seized it and placed it in line at the crime lab behind other rifles being tested.

Investigators had also received a call from a man in the Tucson Psychiatric Institute who claimed he had information about the massacre. He gave his name, Michael McGraw, and hung up. Police found a Michael McGraw, 24, there, but he denied making such a call and insisted that someone else had done it to implicate him. Nevertheless, they interrogated him, and eventually he broke down and confessed to being involved in the temple massacre. He also implicated four other young men: Mark Felix Nunez, 19; Leo Valdez Bruce, 28; Dante Parker, 20; and Victor Zarate, 27. They were brought in and questioned, while their homes were searched. After all four confessed, they were detained for a grand jury hearing.

But then all five recanted and said they had been fed information and coerced, as well as denied access to lawyers. One had a provable alibi, but the other four were detained for trial.

More than a month went by with no new information until October 24, when the Arizona Department of Public Safety ballistics lab reported the results of their analysis of Caratachea's weapon. They had found a match between the casings found in the temple and the ones fired by this .22-caliber semiautomatic Marlin rifle. The task force got a warrant to search the apartment where Jonathan Doody lived with Alessandro "Alex" Garcia. They were companions at Agua Fria High School and fellow air force ROTC students.

The search turned up a 20-guage Stevens shotgun, which was soon matched to the shell casings found at the crime scene. When investigators talked with the families, they learned that Doody's younger brother, David, had been involved at the temple, so he was familiar with it.

The boys were soon arrested, and on November 22, the four innocent men were released. Doody and Garcia made statements that implicated them, although each pointed the finger at the other as the killer. Garcia drew a sketch of the temple to show that he had been there. He got details right, such as the fact that rice had been spilled on the storeroom floor and that the nun's dentures were on a table by her bed. Doody, too, eventually offered a confession, but then got a lawyer, who claimed that his own interrogation had been lengthy and exhausting

A judge decided that that the two boys would be tried as adults, with the potential penalty of death. A year later, in 1993, Garcia struck a plea deal for life in prison in exchange for testifying against Doody. He gave a statement, describing how Doody had shot each victim and had returned to each one to shoot them all again. He also took credit for one more crime for which a mentally retarded man had been coerced to confess and was facing the death penalty. In October 1991, two months after the temple massacre, Garcia and his 14-year-old girlfriend, Michelle Hoover, had murdered Alice Cameron, 50, in a campground. Garcia had goaded Michelle to do it. She pled guilty and got 15 years.

As Garcia went to Doody's trial in May 1993, he revealed his version of what had happened on the night of August 9, 1991. It began as a plan for a robbery. He and Doody had heard from Jonathan's brother about a gold Buddha and a safe containing $2,000. To make it interesting, they turned it into a "war game." They purchased military clothing and gear, Doody borrowed the rifle, and Garcia took his uncle's shotgun. On the evening of August 9, they drove to the temple between 10:00 and 10:30. They burst in, ordering the residents to the floor. The boys arranged their victims into a circle, kneeling and facing one another, and for an hour one held them at gunpoint while the other searched for keys to the safe and committed general vandalism. At one point, a nun came in and they forced her to join the men.

They managed to grab over $2,600 in cash and change, along with cameras and stereo equipment to pawn. Doody wanted to ensure there would be no witnesses. Standing on a couch over his prey, he started shooting them. Garcia joined in, using the shotgun to wound some of them, but he insisted that he had not killed anyone.

In July 12, 1993, Jonathan Doody was convicted of nine murders and eleven other criminal counts, and sentenced to 281 years in prison. Although the prosecutor had sought the death sentence, the judge decided that it was unclear as to which young man had actually pulled the rifle's trigger. Alessandro Garcia was sentenced to 271 years in prison, the maximum possible under his plea agreement.

Some kids just grow up dangerous. They're vulnerable to images of strength that call for proof via destruction. They may exercise this through videogames, role-playing fantasy games, obsessions with some destructive political or religious leader, or interest in organizations that promise secret knowledge and control over others.

A few such children develop the minds of a perpetrator, angry and bent on power, revenge, or the need to express some inner feeling with violence. In France, Eric Borel, a fan of Adolf Hitler and the Nazis, went on a killing spree on September 24, 1995. With a hammer and baseball bat, he bludgeoned to death his mother, stepfather, and brother. Then he armed himself with his hunting rifle and walked six miles into the town square of Cuers. For half an hour in a parking lot, he shot people, killing nine and wounding seven before shooting himself in the head.

Others kids may just be the unstable kind who need to follow someone, and who will even commit murder if the leader says so. Such was said to be the case with the next killing team.

ROLE PLAYING

It was Alex Baranyi who first decided that he would one day kill someone, but his big plans had more to do with his addiction to role-playing games than to any concrete plan to act out. He even scared his best friend, David Anderson—at first. In the end, it appeared from the evidence to be Anderson who led the dance, Anderson who targeted the victims, and Anderson who eventually decided what they were going to do.

On January 3, 1997, in Bellevue, Washington, the two high school dropouts, both 17, massacred the four members of Bill Wilson's family. Their activities were documented in their trial transcripts, the *Seattle Times*, and a book, *Deadly Secrets*, written after the trials by reporter Putsata Reang.

Regardless of who was ultimately responsible for the killing activity, their first act was to lure Kim Wilson, 20, whom they both knew well and with whom Baranyi had once been obsessed, to a local park around midnight. Apparently in the role of their characters in Dungeons & Dragons (Baranyi was "Slicer Thunderclap"), one or both of them strangled her to death, stomped on her ribs, and left her there.

Then the killer or killers went to the Wilson home, where Anderson had been a guest for a while, due to problems he supposedly had with his father. The door was unlocked, as always, so it was easy for them to creep inside while the Wilsons slept. Bill Wilson, his wife, and his other daughter, Julia, had no idea what was coming for them. The events were eventually reported by Baranyi, who refused to implicate Anderson.

He said that he first went into the bedroom and used a baseball bat to beat to death a person lying in the bed, which turned out to be Mrs. Wilson. She never awakened (though he later pierced her neck several times with a long knife), but Mr. Wilson woke up and struggled with Baranyi, so he battered and stabbed the man until he slumped next to the bed. Then Baranyi went into the hall to find Kim's younger sister, Julia. He stabbed her to death as she attempted to defend herself, sticking a small knife into her eye three times for good measure. One of them left a large, clear imprint of a stomper boot on Bill Wilson's shirt. A blood and print match later implicated Anderson.

As typically occurs with team killers, when the heat is on, one invariably breaks down. Often it's the psychopathic person, calculating his advantage by turning in the other, but sometimes he or she has underestimated the breaking point of the follower. In this case, Baranyi confessed first—but he did not betray his idol. He claimed that he had been astounded that they had really set out to murder someone, but that he had done it for a person he would not name. Baranyi took the full blame, saying he did all the killings himself, choking Kim and using a baseball bat on the rest of her family. But then the forensics lab matched evidence that implicated Anderson as well, and he was arrested. Several of his friends and associates admitted to the police that he had often talked about murdering someone, including a family.

Both were tried and convicted of premeditated aggravated murder. From the evidence, it seems that the trigger may have been Kim asking Anderson for money that he owed her. According to the prosecutor, Anderson was used to girls worshipping him, buying him things, and doing anything they could to be in his presence. Kim had given him a deadline, and since it coincided with his desire to kill someone before he reached the age of 18 (mistakenly believing he would not be prosecuted as an adult), she had inadvertently sealed her fate.

Psychologists appeared as expert witnesses in Baranyi's trial. For the defense, Dr. Karen Froming explained that he suffered from bipolar disorder and from low self-esteem, such that he would form an attachment to someone else and might do anything to keep that attachment alive. His abandonment by his parents had affected his ability to feel good about himself, and in addition to that, he had a genetic legacy of depression.

Baranyi, she explained, had difficulty making friends, so when he met Anderson, who included him in a world in which he craved to be involved, Anderson became a symbol of life itself. Baranyi would sacrifice everything for the relationship. Together the boys had developed an elaborate fantasy life involving swordplay, wizards, and dragons. Dr. Froming believed that Baranyi had been following Anderson's directions when he had killed the Wilson family. She did not think he had the capability of forming premeditated intent.

The rebuttal witness for the prosecution was Dr. Robert Wheeler. He had administered the same psychological battery of assessment tests as had Dr. Froming, but had derived a different interpretation. He offered a diagnosis of antisocial personality disorder, which involved being impulsive, aggressive, and lacking in empathy or remorse. He said that Baranyi knew what he was doing—had even admitted as much—and was not suffering from any form of diminished capacity in his reasoning.

No psychological defense was offered for Anderson, since his defense attorneys throughout several trials relied on a lack of physical evidence to prove he was not part of the deadly scheme. In the end, both boys lost.

It came as no surprise to the public at large that some children were violent. By the time the trials were concluded, there had already been several school shootings that commanded headlines across the country.

CONTAGION

In the late 1990s, it seemed that an epidemic had hit American schools. Children were acquiring guns and bombs, and then going to school to kill teachers and classmates. Some were reacting, some were making "statements," and some were just doing whatever seemed to relieve a stressful situation. In 1979, Brenda Spencer, 16, killed two adults and wounded nine elementary school children when she decided that shooting at them with her new .22 semiautomatic rifle was a good way to cut through a Monday's boredom. Different cultural influences were targeted for blame for these aggressive children, from violent films to music videos to videogames. Clifford Linedecker documents them all in *Babyface Killers*, and each was covered extensively in the national media. Linedecker lists thirty-one separate incidents between 1979 and 1999, for reasons ranging from anger over bad grades to plans to take over the school.

While there were shootings during the 1980s and early 1990s, the massacre-minded killers who grabbed widespread attention seemed to get a real foothold in 1996 when Barry Loukaitis, 14, dressed like a gunslinger and went into class in Moses Lake, Washington. Concealed in his long duster were two pistols, seventy-eight rounds of ammunition, and a high-powered rifle. He killed two students and a teacher, and wounded another student. A month later, David Dubose Jr., 16, killed a teacher in a school hallway in Atlanta, Georgia.

A year passed and then Evan Ramsey, 16 and feeling bullied, went to Bethel High School in Alaska with a shotgun. He killed a boy with whom he'd argued and then injured two other students. Then he went to the administration office and shot the principal, Ron Edwards, killing him. Two 14-year-old friends were arrested as accomplices.

Other kids paid attention. On October 1, 1997, Luke Woodham, 16, felt enraged when his girlfriend in Pearl, Mississippi, broke up with him. He stabbed his mother that morning and went to school with a rifle and a pistol. There, he killed his former girlfriend and another girl. Seven other students were wounded before he ran out of ammunition and was disarmed. He complained that the world had wronged him and he just couldn't take it anymore. He eventually blamed demons.

Two months later in Paducah, Kentucky, Michael Carneal, 14, opened fire on a small prayer group. Three girls died and five students were wounded. When Carneal was stopped, he had a pistol, two rifles, and two shotguns, along with 700 rounds of ammunition, all of it stolen. He'd threatened earlier to "shoot up" the school, but no one had taken him seriously.

Less than four months went by before a pair of kids—the youngest yet—shocked the nation. Andrew Golden, 11, and his gun buddy, Mitchell Johnson, 13, dressed in camouflage fatigues on March 24, 1998, and gunned down fifteen people at the Westside Middle School playground in Jonesboro, Arkansas. Five died, all of them female, and four were children. The boys had a van stocked full of ammunition and guns, which they took from their kin. Golden went into the school and set off a fire alarm, then ran to join Johnson. As people filed out for the fire drill, the boys began shooting.

A month later, to the day, Andrew J. Wurst, 14, took a pistol into the eighth-grade graduation dance in Edinboro, Pennsylvania, and killed a popular teacher. Then he opened fire into the crowd, wounding another teacher and two classmates.

Another month went by and 15-year-old Kipland Kinkel carried out a shooting on May 21. He had just been expelled from school in Springfield, Oregon, for having a gun in school. He returned the following day with a semiautomatic rifle and went into the cafeteria, where he killed one student and wounded eight others, one of whom later died. The stampede hurt fifteen more. Kinkel was disarmed and taken to the police station, where he withdrew a hidden knife. He claimed he wanted to die and told the police, "Just kill me."

It turned out that he had good reason. Police officers who went to his home discovered that he'd also shot both of his parents and booby-trapped the house with five homemade bombs—one of which he'd placed beneath his mother's corpse. There have been several detailed examinations of his case, because he came from a home in which both parents were teachers and much time had been spent trying to help him navigate the perils of adolescence. The shooting spree seemed to have no clear cause. According to Kinkel, he was terrified of what his father would say about his being expelled from school. He believed he had nowhere to turn and no choice but to end his parents' lives.

Child psychologist Jonathan Kellerman, author of *Savage Spawn: Reflections on Violent Children,* includes Kinkel on a list of violent kids. He thinks that the crime showed a finely honed sense of premeditation, and in fact, over the previous few years, Kinkel had been arming himself with numerous guns and explosives. "What turns them on," says Kellerman about these aggressive children, "is the kick, the high, the slaking of impulse . . . the subjugation of the rest of us."[1] They can seem quiet, but that may in fact be the emotional flatness that signals psychopathy. A good predictor of dangerousness in children, Kellerman states, is the combination of a certain temperament with a chaotic environment.

Yet Kinkel did not come from a chaotic home. He lived in "Shangri-la," his parents' luxury home deep in the quiet Oregon woods. He'd grown up with a talented and loving sister, and caring parents. Nevertheless, he decided that he wanted others to view him as "dangerous." He hung out with kids involved in petty theft. He framed the lyrics from Marilyn Manson's song "The Reflecting God," to the effect that there was "no salvation," and became fascinated with explosives. He also collected guns, hiding his stash from his parents.

In 1999, PBS's *Frontline* program produced a documentary, "The Killer at Thurston High." That crew interviewed Kinkel's friends, school personnel, and even his sister, Kristin, to try to learn the answer as to why he'd turned to such wanton violence. While there is no formula for knowing exactly what goes wrong in the life of a kid, there appear to be several factors that joined in Kinkel's life in just the wrong way—factors not true for his sister, although she was raised in the same home.

He experienced a number of episodes in which he had failed and felt his father's disappointment—perhaps more heavily than he should have. He was dyslexic, athletically clumsy, small, and weak, with poor skills for managing his anger. To vent his feelings, he set off explosives, which taught him what "worked." It made him feel better and gave him a sense of mastery over something. His parents, and later his therapist, gave him mixed messages about guns. His parents also argued over sending him to therapy. He began taking Prozac for depression, but when he was doing better, he stopped. He fell in love and then lost the girl. He became obsessed with the soundtrack for the film version of *Romeo and Juliet*, which starred Leonardo DiCaprio and in which violence and suicide are highly glamorized. He had also gotten into trouble for tossing rocks at cars from an overpass—a felony.

In short, he had a burden of disappointment and a clandestine life of power and success from those things that made him both more dangerous and more likely to turn to violence if cornered.

As Kinkel left his home, with his deceased parents inside, he turned on the *Romeo and Juliet* soundtrack, set it to play continuously, and left a note: "I have killed my parents. I am a horrible son." In his journal, he'd written, "My head just doesn't work right. Goddam these voices in my head." (It should be noted here that Luke Woodham had already expressed that voices had told him to kill, quoted by national media. In no records or therapeutic notes has the idea that Kinkel might be schizophrenic been raised.) Then he went to school with his rifle and a pistol, and in less than a minute shot forty-eight rounds into his classmates. When taken into custody and questioned about why he'd done this, he just kept saying through tears, as caught on footage shown in the documentary, "I had no other choice . . . I had to."

Though he was 15, Kinkel was certified to be tried as an adult. He'd initiated an insanity defense, but dropped it. During the sentencing phase, a brain scan was introduced as evidence in his favor, and Dr. Richard Konkel, a neurologist, testified that it supposedly showed areas of decreased activity consistent with recent research on childhood schizophrenia. Thus he was likely susceptible to a psychotic episode.

Kinkel pleaded guilty to four counts of first-degree murder and twenty-four counts of attempted murder. He was sentenced to 112 years in prison without parole. During that time a debate transpired, which continues today, regarding his mental state and the influences that may lead to juvenile violence.

Dr. Pamela Blake reviewed the brain scans of thirty-one murderers, and twenty had evidence of frontal-lobe dysfunction. At the very least, this dysfunction was implicated in poor impulse control and violent outbursts. Teachers had described Kinkel as a kid who easily lost his temper when provoked. Blake indicated that this was true of someone with brain damage (although she did not address the question of whether this could be true of someone without brain damage).

In the *Journal of Biological Psychiatry* in 1997, researchers had indicated that six areas of the brain were implicated in violence. Yet another group of researchers said in the *American Journal of Psychiatry* that some sort of attachment disorder—neglect or rejection by the mother, for example—is required to predispose the abnormal brain toward violence. Dr. Adrian Raine from the University of Southern California directed both studies. The brains of forty-one murderers who had pleaded not guilty by reason of insanity were scanned. Control subjects were matched for age and gender. Positron emission tomography scans measured the uptake (fuel for cellular activity) of sugar during simple tasks, and the group of murderers showed significantly lower rates of glucose uptake in the prefrontal cortex, the corpus callosum, and the posterior parietal cortex. They also had weaker activity in the amygdala and hippocampus in the left hemisphere, with stronger activity in the thalamus, amygdala, and hypothalamus of the right hemisphere.

In other words, poor functioning in some areas indicates an inability to learn from experience, as well as an emotional load that outweighs the ability of the left hemisphere to regulate it. Added to that, another study indicated that boys who had experienced maternal rejection were twice as likely as boys who had not to get involved in violent crime.

Even so, there was no evidence of maternal rejection in Kinkel's case, and too little is known about the brains of other school shooters to apply these findings. The researchers suggested that prenatal care and parenting skills may need more attention than they're currently getting.

The year after Kinkel's violent episode, an even more shocking event took place, implicating yet another potential causal factor: fringe groups and violent videogames.

DEADLY INTENT

On April 20, 1999, on the anniversary of Adolf Hitler's birthday in 1889, school killings reached their apex with the tragedy at Columbine High School in Littleton, Colorado.

Dylan Klebold, 17, and Eric Harris, 18, had a plan. Immersed in violent videogames and paramilitary techniques, they spent a year collecting an arsenal of semiautomatic guns and homemade bombs with which to perpetrate a crime that the nation would never forget—and they succeeded. The massacre at Columbine is still marked as the pinnacle of the school shooting episodes.

Ironically, they had a getaway plan: if they actually succeeded and did not have to kill themselves, they would steal a plane to fly to an island; if caught, they would fly it instead into some building in New York. (The September 11, 2001, massacre via similar means was two years away, but Klebold was actually born on September 11 in 1981.)

The two boys were said to be members of "the Trenchcoat Mafia," dubbed for their habit of wearing long black trench coats. They had long been bullied by classmates, sometimes in most distasteful and shameful ways. Understandably, they did not care for such treatment, although they apparently adopted an indifferent attitude. Little did anyone know what they had in mind. Having no particular reason to live, by some accounts, they decided to take out as many of their hated classmates as they could and, in the process, blow up the school. They might live or die; they did not seem to care which.

The day before their rampage, they sent an e-mail to the local police declaring the plan for their revenge. They blamed parents and teachers for turning their children into intolerant sheep and announced their own suicide. It was a disturbing forewarning. At 11:30 A.M. on April 20, 1999, they hid weapons and bombs beneath their coats and then ran through the school, yelling and shooting. When they reached the library, they cornered and killed several students before turning their weapons on themselves. It all happened quickly, but with devastating impact. After police got into the building, they counted thirty-four casualties and fifteen people dead, including the shooters.

Then Harris's diary turned up, which confirmed the elaborate plan. For over a year they had worked at it, drawing maps, collecting weapons, and devising a system of silent hand signals for coordinating their moves. Behind closed doors in their parents' homes, they had spoken of death. The simple fact that emerged was that they were angry, bitter kids who had access to guns. For them, what the culture viewed as evil—shooting people—was a positive means for disturbing the social status quo.

Dr. Park Dietz and his associates from TAG (Threat Assessment Group) came to Littleton after the massacre to carry out what they called a psychiatric autopsy, which they filmed for the A&E Network. While they looked into the boys' records for information about anger management and other incidents leading up to the killings, they were unable to speak to the boys' families, which left gaping holes in their assessments. They concluded that both boys had suffered from depression, one of them more than the other, and that their association with each other had given them the courage to carry out their plan.

Then came the copycat incidents. It wasn't long before some kids decided to "out-Columbine Columbine" and blow up their schools or start shooting during an assembly. But by now, classmates were getting savvy and turning in these would-be assassins. No longer was it believed that kids who made such threats were harmless or "just kidding." At times, this caution went overboard, and kids who did not deserve it were expelled, but other kids were also stopped in their tracks before anyone got hurt.

An unnamed boy in North Carolina who kept a "corpse list" and who plotted to blow up his high school with homemade napalm was arrested and charged as a juvenile. Two high school students were arrested in Louisiana for planning to re-create Columbine on its fifth anniversary. They had drawings of themselves celebrating on a school roof, while bloody bodies hung out windows below. In Sunrise, Florida, a 13-year-old girl was charged with crafting a shooting scheme. Three days after the Columbine incident, she had met with friends to reveal a map of the school's surveillance system. Then she showed them a hit list that included the names of nine students and school personnel. In Hoyt, Kansas, in 2001, three students who admired the Columbine killers were arrested for planning an attack, and they had the means to do it.

Many of these children expressed anger over having been bullied or rejected. A study published in 1999 indicates that children who expect to be rejected tend to perceive more hostility and rejection in ambiguous comments than those who are not so sensitive. Such children then behave aggressively and experience increased interpersonal difficulties, along with declining social functioning. That makes them get rejected more often, so they become further distressed.

However, it takes more than just feelings of hostility to form a plan to kill someone—particularly if you have a number of people in mind as targets. Psychologists Derek Miller and John Looney had studied adolescent killers back in the 1970s and noted that they often showed a capacity to dehumanize others. Those at high risk to kill saw others as objects that thwarted them. This perspective was thought to have developed from the way these kids had themselves been dehumanized. They did not view themselves as valuable, so it was possible that they could not view others as valuable. In fact, the extent to which they were dehumanized seemed to be a measure of the likelihood that they would do the same to others.

In April 2000, marking the first anniversary of the Columbine tragedy, the *New York Times* published a series about violence that was based on one hundred cases of American rampage killers from the past fifty years. It was noted that the incident in Littleton, Colorado, was one of thirteen for the year 1999. Rampage killers, according to this study, tend to be better educated than typical murderers, are likely to have military experience, and are more likely to kill themselves. The most significant influence on their outbursts appears to have been some form of mental illness. One-third had histories of violence and half had made threats. Most attacks were the result of a buildup over time of rage and the effects of depression, and more than half had been able to purchase guns easily.

Of the 100 kids documented in the study, nineteen were teenagers, and they showed a pattern that set them apart from the adults:

- While adults tend to act alone, kids often act with the support of their peers.
- Kids may try to collaborate and get others involved, and some of them kill together.
- They will often boast of their plans to their peers.
- While mental health problems are common, fewer kids than adults commit suicide.
- The youngest killers are less emotionally detached than older ones.
- Most kids involved in school violence are white and prefer (and somehow acquire) semiautomatic weapons. Almost half of the kids studied had shown some evidence of mental disturbance, including delusions and hallucinations.

Any pattern of behavior that persists over time tends to intensify. This does not necessarily mean that a bully will become a school killer, but it means that kids who develop an obsession with weapons or violent games, and who tend to threaten violence, are more likely to eventually act out than those who don't. Some of the behaviors to be especially concerned about include an increase in deception, blaming others, avoiding responsibility, avoiding efforts to achieve goals, using intimidation to control others, showing lack of empathy for others, exploiting others' weaknesses, a pattern of overreacting or of anger, being depressed or withdrawn, carrying weapons, complaints about loneliness, and having excessive television or videogame habits—three or more hours a day.

In fact, a publication in *Psychiatric Times* in October 2001 indicated that three decades of research implicated television violence in the higher incidences of crimes. Dr. John P. Murray says that viewers of violent television are influenced in several areas, notably in increased aggression to solve conflicts, desensitization to violence, and fear of becoming a victim. In preliminary research, they mapped the brain activity of eight children watching violent programs—for example, boxing scenes from the film *Rocky IV*. They compared this with nonviolent programming, and found that violent programs "recruited" numerous structures in the right hemisphere, including the amygdala, hippocampus, and premotor cortex.

All were areas involved in arousal, memory and attention, or detection of threat. The research suggested significant emotional processing and memory storage of video violence. The study suggested areas for further attention.

Another study at the Indiana School of Medicine conducted over a period of two years and published in 2002 indicated that violent media affected aggressive children with disruptive disorders (rule breaking, resistance, and destructive acts) differently than nonaggressive children. Via fMRI scans, the aggressive children were shown to have different frontal lobe activation patterns, showing less behavioral control.

Dr. William G. Kronenberger stated on the university's Web site that "this is the first evidence that adolescents with aggressive, disruptive behavior disorders have brain activation patterns that are different from non-aggressive adolescents while watching violent videogames."[2] He went on to indicate that there appeared to be a difference, depending on amount of past exposure to violent videos, to the way the brain responded.

It's clear that we need to develop better ways of dealing with kids who view violence as the best means for solving their problems. It's also clear that we need to encourage students who hear one of their friends make a threat to take it seriously, even if they don't believe that this person would ever really follow through. Bullying by peers may never be eradicated, but listening to kids whose manner of processing such taunts is disturbed may be the only way to develop appropriate interventions and stop the violence. It's got to be treated on the inside rather than through external controls, because kids who feel resentful and angry, and who view the world in violent terms, will always find some way to act out.

And some of them hold the anger until they become adults . . . with families.

CHAPTER 6

Family Massacres

ANNIHILATION

On March 12, 2003, in Fresno, California, police officers responded to a phone call from two women who were trying to get into the home of Marcus Wesson, 57, to get access to their children. The women had given up custody to Wesson and now wanted their children back, but he had refused to let them in. The police arrived and ordered Wesson to come out of the house, but he ignored them. Instead he ran into a back bedroom, as two more women came out of the home. Associated Press news reports stated that these four women were Wesson's girlfriends or wives and the mothers of the children inside.

A neighbor said that just before the police arrived he heard gunshots. Wesson surrendered, presenting himself as a man with dreadlocks down to his knees and stained with what appeared to be blood. Then the police went in.

To their horror, in one room they found twelve coffins stacked against a wall and in a back bedroom nine bodies on top of one another and intertwined with piles of clothing. One was an adult woman, another was a 17-year-old girl, and the rest were children from ages 1 to 8. Two of those were just babies, and it turned out that they were Wesson's children by incest with his own daughters. The eight children had been fathered with six different women and had been home-schooled, apparently to keep them under his control. As sinister as the coffins seemed, an antiques dealer said that Wesson had bought them five years earlier, allegedly to use the wood for houseboat repair.

Detectives arrived with a search warrant and went in to look for evidence as to what had occurred and why. A coroner's report issued a few days later revealed that the victims had all been shot to death. As to what may have triggered the sudden slaughter, Wesson had been given a citation for living in a building zoned for commercial use and was to pay a fine or get a special permit. On the day he was supposed to comply, he may have killed his family, or ordered them to die. After his arrest, he was held on $9 million bail.

A lawyer who had some acquaintance with Wesson said that the women in his company wore scarves and dark robes, and seemed to comply with whatever he wanted. They also supported him. He allegedly ran the family with an iron will. One news report claimed that Wesson told police that he killed his children to prevent them from being taken from him. He had two surviving sons, ages 29 and 19, and they did not believe the reports. Other people who knew him asked that the police forbid him phone calls in jail, because they feared he would command his entire family to destroy themselves—and that they would do it. A fan of David Koresh, who had kept strict control over his followers in a religious cult in Waco, Texas, also doomed to die together, Wesson apparently believed that he could order his wives and children to operate according to his dictates.

As more facts came out, Wesson was charged with more counts alleging long-term sexual abuse going back to 1988. He was also charged with forcible rape of females living with him, allegedly with at least five victims under the age of 14. Yet his defense attorney told Associated Press reporters that in fact one of the victims may have killed the others and herself. Beneath the body of Wesson's 25-year-old daughter, mother of one of his children, lay a hunting knife and a .22-caliber gun. A bullet had entered her eye at an upward angle, consistent with suicide, and while prosecutors insisted that the evidence pointed to Wesson, sources close to the family indicated that he may have commanded his daughter to do it. As of this writing, the results of this case were pending. A judge determined there was sufficient evidence for Wesson to go to trial, and the prosecutors subsequently announced that they would seek the death penalty.

Most family mass murders are committed by men. Often, the point for them is to wipe out the family they have produced, perhaps to annihilate any trace of themselves or perhaps to start over. It may be the final point on a long road of frustration, but as in the Wesson case, it may be something as simple as a threat to one's sense of control. Often this occurs during custody disputes, such as the following case.

In what newspapers described as a "rifle rampage," George Banks, a prison guard dressed in army fatigues and carrying a semiautomatic AR-15 rifle, began eliminating his family around 2:00 A.M. on September 25, 1982, in Wilkes-Barre, Pennsylvania. Two stepchildren who survived actually witnessed the horror as he broke into their trailer and killed their mother, grandmother, sister, and half brother. They survived because they hid. That same night he killed nine others, including a man who was just standing outside the home where the slaughter took place. He also shot another bystander, who survived.

After Banks was arrested and arraigned, his attorney indicated that he was mentally incompetent. At the time of the shooting, Banks was on leave from his job because he had threatened to commit suicide and had expressed some paranoid ideation about his food being poisoned. He was having trouble finding work.

Dr. Michael J. Spodak, chief of psychiatry at Baltimore County General Hospital in Maryland, had examined the defendant for his competence to stand trial and found him remorseful over killing his children but preoccupied with conspiracy issues. Spodak thought Banks was out of touch with reality and irrational. "He said he thinks someone moved the bodies around," Spodak commented to reporters for local papers, "and put extra bullets into them and changed some of the clothes."[1] He diagnosed Banks as "terminally paranoid" and incompetent to stand trial.

However, Dr. Robert Sadoff had also examined the subject for the prosecution and said that while Banks acted in a strange manner, he did understand the charges against him. The judge declared him competent and the trial was on. Jurors were imported from across the state in Pittsburgh. They heard how Banks was the child of a black father and white mother and although he was married to a black woman who had separated from him, at the time of the crime he had lived with three white women in a rundown house. In all, he had killed four women with whom he'd had children, seven children (five were his), an elderly woman, and a stranger. Associates indicated that he hated both races whose heritage he shared. He did not like being pushed around and had said things that suggested he felt persecuted by whites and blacks alike. He had been in a dispute over child custody with the woman in the trailer home and had a history of battering the other women.

Despite testimony about Banks's paranoia, his bizarre statements, and his alleged motive of sparing his children from the racial biases he had suffered, the jury convicted him of twelve counts of first-degree murder and sentenced him to death for each. In 2001 his death sentence was overturned on a technicality and in 2004 his case went to the Supreme Court.

As horrendous as these crimes were, in a just a few years, another man would surpass them.

OVERWHELMING NEED FOR CONTROL

When Ronald Gene Simmons, 47, gunned down several people on the morning of December 28, 1987, in Russellville, Arkansas, he was winding down. What appeared to have been an incident of workplace violence was far worse.

His story is told in *Zero at the Bone*, by Bryce Marshall and Paul Williams. With a .22-caliber pistol, he shot a receptionist at a law office in the head, and then moved on to the Taylor Oil Company. He shot two men there and two more in a nearby convenience store. He ended his spree in the Woodline Motor Freight Company, where he wounded a woman and took another hostage. The police arrived and Simmons gave up peacefully.

They learned that Simmons had become infatuated with receptionist Kathy Kendrick, 25, and that she had resisted him, so they assumed his shooting was triggered by revenge. Investigators learned where Simmons lived outside town, so they went to notify his family. When no one answered and the place seemed eerily still, they entered the home through a window.

Inside the place, which was decorated for Christmas, Simmons's son, daughter, and their spouses had been shot and lay dead. His granddaughter, age 6, appeared to have been smothered to death. The officers returned to town to get more resources for searching the thirteen-acre property.

The next day, investigators came across disturbed earth over which lay barbed wire and a piece of sheet metal. They dug down and unearthed a body. Then another. They kept digging until they had found the remains of seven people just barely covered by dirt. Here were Simmons's wife, two of his sons, three daughters, and his 3-year-old granddaughter. Another team found two more corpses closed in the trunks of junked cars: Simmons's infant grandsons.

All of the adults had been shot, while the children had been asphyxiated in some manner. A coroner determined that they had been killed a few days earlier, just before Christmas. Simmons gained the notoriety in that moment of having committed the largest family massacre in the country. All those who had lived under Simmons's roof, as well as grown children who had returned for the holidays, were now dead.

Simmons was charged with sixteen counts of first-degree murder and four counts of attempted murder. He was taken for a psychiatric examination. Simmons had been obsessed with order and control, had kept his family captive in a run-down house, and had been abusing his wife and daughters. No mail came for them, no calls, and no friends. They lived amid a heap of junked cars and unfinished projects.

The reason for that apparently lay in Simmons's flight from the law in New Mexico, where he was wanted on charges of incest. He had impregnated his 15-year-old daughter, Sheila, and before he could be arrested, he had fled with his family to Arkansas. Then the daughter he had raped got married and left. One of the "granddaughters" he had killed was his own daughter, born of incest. He had been in love with Sheila and had felt that she'd betrayed him.

Despite having hallucinations while incarcerated, Simmons was declared competent to stand trial and was convicted of the two murders in town. He resisted the insanity defense, because he did not wish to be locked up. He wanted to be executed, and hoped for that before going to trial for killing his family. However, he was not shown this mercy. He was held in prison until he could be tried for the horrendous familicide, and he was sentenced once again to death. He told the jury they had done the right thing and refused to appeal his sentence, so on June 25, 1990, he was given a lethal injection.

STARTING OVER

Statistics from the U.S. Department of Justice suggest that approximately one-third of intrafamilial killings are done by women, who are also responsible for more than 50 percent of the murders of children. Nevertheless, when it comes to wiping out an entire family, fathers lead the pack.

In a famous case that occurred in November 1971, John Emil List systematically slaughtered his wife, mother, two sons, and daughter in his mansion in Westfield, New Jersey. He pulled them into the ballroom to place them on sleeping bags, cleaned up the place, and turned on a phonograph that would play church music repetitively. Leaving all the lights on and writing out a long confession, he slipped away.

The List case has been described in many sources, from *America's Most Wanted* to *Time* magazine to books like *Thou Shalt Not Kill* and *Death Sentence*.

A month went by before the authorities found the corpses. Apparently List believed he had done his family a favor, sending their souls to heaven. More likely it was the cowardly act of a man who had lost his job, accumulated debt, and could not face failure. In any event, clearly he became a fugitive who would elude law enforcement for eighteen years.

America's Most Wanted decided to air the case in 1989, presenting a sculpted bust of what List would look like that many years later. A former neighbor of a man named Bob Clark called in. She recognized him as John List.

Ten days later, FBI agents located "Bob Clark" at his office, proved he was List, and arrested him. List was convicted of five counts of first-degree murder and sentenced to life in prison. When he was interviewed a decade later, he appeared to have little remorse about what he had done.

Adolescent sons are next on the list of those most likely to massacre their entire family, and some, while adults, are still living in an adolescent phase by remaining at home and being supported by their parents.

In Amityville, New York, a family massacre was carried out one night that would make the place and the crime famous well beyond that neighborhood. Ronald "Butch" DeFeo Jr., 23, grew up in an affluent home. On November 13, 1974, at approximately 3:00 A.M., he took a .35-caliber lever-action Marlin rifle and murdered his father, mother, two sisters, and two brothers in their beds. The youngest was 9. Butch then removed his clothing, bathed, and redressed. He cleaned up the crime scene, picking up cartridges and stuffing them with his bloody clothing into a pillowcase. This he stuffed into a sewer on his way to work; he tossed the rifle into a canal.

That evening, he called the police to report that his family had been murdered, and hinted at the Mafia's involvement. Then his story changed, and it was not long before he became the primary suspect. And still his story shifted and changed.

For a psychiatrist, he admitted to (or faked having had) blackouts in which he did things that he did not recall. Eventually he said he had done the whole thing out of self-defense during a violent family argument, and then that it was his sister who had done it with his gun. Finally, he claimed that the police had coerced a false confession out of him. Ultimately he said that he had killed because he was God, and he pleaded not guilty by reason if insanity. Apparently he was hoping to beat the rap and end up with the family money.

Dr. Daniel Schwartz, a psychiatrist, affirmed the delusions and Butch's belief that his family had it in for him. He had acted out against them while in a psychotic state and could not be held responsible for his actions. Schwartz relied on Butch's self-report that he had not heard the gun firing as evidence of psychotic dissociation, and denied that he could be malingering. He had carried out the executions without feeling, so he had to be insane. His attempt to hide the evidence was just irrational.

There was also a psychiatrist for the prosecution: Dr. Harold Zolan. He diagnosed Butch as having antisocial personality disorder, which was not the same as being psychotic. He knew right from wrong and appreciated the consequences of his act; hence he had hidden the evidence that linked him to the crimes. His psychiatric record from adolescence indicated that he was passive-aggressive and socially impotent.

After the murders, Butch drew up a long list of fifty other people he wished to kill. He repeatedly indicated that he had no feelings about killing his family aside from being glad or relieved they were gone. While some professionals who had studied the case indicate that family violence and the modeling of deception and theft may have been responsible for Butch's slaughter, in truth no one really knows.

The house was sold and it ended up being the setting for another fraud, *The Amityville Horror,* a book and movie based on the idea that the house had been built on an Indian burial ground and that the restless spirits had caused anyone who lived there to become insanely violent.

A few sons, like James Ruppert, bide their time into later adulthood before they kill. Ruppert was living with his mother in Hamilton, Ohio. People considered him to be quiet, helpful, and responsible. The day after he turned 41, in 1975, was Easter Sunday. Relatives were coming over for a holiday dinner. As everyone gathered to eat, Ruppert armed himself in his room with three revolvers and a rifle. He propped the rifle up in the kitchen and systematically began to eliminate each member of his family. Ten of the eleven victims were shot in the head and one in the chest.

Ruppert called the police himself but would not talk. After he was charged, he pleaded not guilty by reason of insanity. The crime scene was locked up and it remained that way for a year.

Ruppert's attorney said that for the past decade Ruppert had been psychotic and therefore was incapable of controlling his actions. Psychiatrists said on his behalf that he had been obsessed with the belief that his family was involved in a conspiracy with the police against him. In his self-report (which cannot be entirely trusted), he said that his mother and brother had brutalized him most of his life. He had been unable to see others in any other light than suspicion and fear. Increasingly, he had been consumed with rage and it had built to the point where he had acted out compulsively, for no apparent reason.

The prosecutors were prepared for this line of defense. They called witnesses who helped them to piece together an entirely different scenario—one based in greed and a full awareness of what he was doing. They indicated that the unemployed Ruppert, with a history of failed investments and indebtedness, had hoped to collect $300,000 by pretending to be psychotic and then going through the mental health system quickly. It came out that his mother was close to asking him to leave her home. Three mental health experts testified that he had known what he was doing.

Yet there were clear records of his paranoia and aggressiveness before the murders. He believed the police and private detectives were following him and that the FBI was tapping his phone. It's also true that there was clear evidence that he preplanned the massacre. Two months prior, he had requested a silencer, and two days before, he had been shooting his gun in a remote area. He had told a female friend that he had a "problem" that needed to be taken care of. She knew that his mother had insisted that he start paying rent, though he had no job and no money.

The three judges agreed with the prosecution: Ruppert was aware of what he was doing and had been able to control his behavior. He was guilty of murder and sentenced to Ohio State Penitentiary. On a technicality, he was granted a new trial in 1982. Another three-judge panel found him guilty in the deaths of his mother and brother, but not guilty by reason of insanity in the other nine murders. In other words, they believed he had a clear motive for the first two, so he was sane, but no real motive for the others, so he was insane. As bizarre as it seems that someone could be found both sane and insane for different facets of the same incident, that was the judgment. He still got two life terms and no inheritance.

His parole hearing came up in 1995. The board rejected his request, sending the killer back to prison. He will not be eligible again until 2035.

FAMILICIDE

Gillian Flaccus reports in a 2003 Associated Press article, "Experts: Oregon fits Familicide Profile," that during the past decade, there have been an average of fifty familicides per year in the United States. In *Fatal Families*, attorney and forensic psychologist Charles Ewing devotes a chapter to familicide, and on his list are the following cases:

1. In 1989, Robert Lynch owned a business that went into decline. He went into debt, but then his wife got pregnant with their fourth child. Unable to cope, he shot them all and killed himself.

2. Bruce Sweazy had been laid off and had reached the point of being suicidal. He got a prescription for an antidepressant, which he declined to take. Then one day in 1994, he used a long-handled axe to hack his wife and three sons to death before shooting himself in the chest.

3. A doctor in Philadelphia, Anthony Paul, had a severely arthritic wife, a retarded and asthmatic daughter, and a healthy son. To end the sufferings of the family, he planned a suicide pact with the three unwilling victims and then administered a lethal dose of medication before killing himself.

Despite the differences in these scenarios, there is a common profile of a man who kills his wife and children. Most killers who fit this profile are white males in their 30s or 40s who react badly to stress and who view their families as extensions of themselves. They typically use a firearm or knife that they have owned for some time. Often they're depressed or intoxicated. Invariably they're described as controlling.

Many experts on the subject of such massacres offer a list of reasons why men might eliminate their families, which tend to range from losing control over family circumstances, with accompanying panic over powerlessness, to seeing only adverse circumstances ahead for themselves or their family members. Such men tend to feel overwhelmed and unable to let their families live while they die. Some just believe that the murders are a necessary sacrifice, or believe that their children cannot survive without them. In a few instances, we find men killing children to get revenge against an estranged wife, or to teach her a lesson, or they may be grieving over losing the family in a divorce. While some may be psychotic, such as Bob Rowe, who used a bat to kill his wife and three children on Long Island, a few have committed the crime as a way to free themselves and make their own lives better. Some report that they feel a duty to the family to kill them in adverse circumstances, while some cases appear to be a sort of suicide by proxy, done within a state of depression. Some men just cannot adjust to being a parent.

J. Reid Meloy, a forensic psychologist and author of *Violent Attachments*, says that such crimes occur as the result of a buildup of anger and frustration, which undermines their already-fragile sense of self. They don't take failure lightly and cannot tolerate humiliation. Having no way to relieve their stress, they let psychological steam build until it just explodes into violence. Their families are generally the easiest target and they have no inner defense against the flow of rage. Once it's done, they return to a sense of equilibrium.

In one of the most bizarre series of familicides, three that occurred in Oregon within a year of one another, it almost appears that there was a contagion effect. Christian and Mary Longo had three children, a boy and two girls. Longo had trouble supporting the family and one day they all just disappeared. On December 19, 2001, the body of Zachary Longo was pulled out of the water of Alsea Bay. Sadie Ann was soon found and then, a week later, Mary and the baby.

Longo was located in a grass hut in Tulum, Mexico, and arrested. He said that he had been "disfellowshipped" by his church and he had no money, so things had been looking bleak. He had not wanted his family to suffer. Longo, who was described by a psychiatrist as narcissistic, was convicted of the charges and sentenced to death.

Less than three months after his family was found dead, in March 2002 the community of McMinnville, just south of Portland, was shaken when a family of six was found shot dead in their home. Landscaping contractor Robert Bryant apparently shot his wife, Janet, and their four children before turning the shotgun on himself. Like the Longos, this family had belonged to the Jehovah's Witness faith, but reportedly had been shunned by their former community for conduct not in harmony with the religion's principles.

Bryant was described as deeply religious and devoted to his family, so the massacre came as a surprise. Nothing appeared to be so stressful in his life as to inspire such an act, except for rumors that he feared that relatives who belonged to the church would sue for custody of his children. The day he shot everyone was his and Janet's seventeenth wedding anniversary.

Nine months later, Edward Morris, 37, killed his pregnant wife and three young children. A hunter found their bodies in Oregon's Tillamook State Forest. Morris's wife and two sons had been shot, his 8-year-old daughter stabbed eighteen times. Morris had fled, but after an international manhunt he was caught in Baker City, Oregon. He, too, had been on the brink of financial ruin. He, too, was deeply religious, but as an evangelical Christian. He so hated violence that he had home-schooled his children to keep them away from disruptions at school. During pretrial evaluations, he said that he'd been plagued by the voices of demons and had struggled against them, but they had told him to kill.

These three are examples of men who sought structure in their lives and, failing to find it, fell apart and targeted those close to them whom they once loved but who had become burdens. And it's not just males who do this. Though rare, some females will wipe out their families as well, although they tend to target only the children.

THE FEMALE ANNIHILATOR

Around 10:00 in the morning on June 20, 2001, Rusty Yates received a call from his wife, Andrea, whom he had left an hour before. She told him that he needed to come home. In light of her recent illness, he asked her to explain and she said, "It's the children." He asked which one, and she told him, "All of them."

The police and ambulance were already at their Houston, Texas, home. John Cannon, the police spokesperson, described for the media what the team had found upon arrival. On a double bed in a back master bedroom, four children were laid out beneath a sheet, clothed and soaking wet. All of them were dead, their eyes wide open. In the bathtub, a young boy was submerged amid feces and vomit that floated on the surface. He looked to be the oldest and he was also dead.

Their mother was Andrea Pia Yates, 36. The primary question was whether or not she had killed the children while in a state of psychosis or had knowingly done it to escape a life she hated. Andrea and Russell had married in 1993, and after the birth of their first child a year later, she began to have violent visions of someone being stabbed. However, she and her husband had Bible-inspired notions about family and motherhood, so she kept her secrets to herself.

Rusty introduced Andrea to a preacher who had impressed him in college, a man named Michael Woroniecki. He was a sharp-witted, sharp-tongued, self-proclaimed "prophet" who preached a simple message about following Jesus but who was so belligerent in public about sinners going to hell (which included most people) that he was often in trouble with various officials for minor violations.

According to a former follower, the religion preached by the Woronieckis involves the idea that women have Eve's witch nature and need to be subservient to men. The preacher judged harshly those mothers who were permissive and who allowed their children to go in the wrong direction. In other words, if the mother was going to hell for some reason, so would the children. They thought it was better to kill oneself than to mislead a child in the way of Jesus—a sentiment Andrea would repeat later in prison interviews.

Andrea had home-schooled her children, but in her fragile mental condition the pressure eventually took its toll. Once a high school valedictorian and high achiever in college, Andrea sank into a deep depression as her family grew. In 1999, she tried to kill herself with a drug overdose, and Russell got her into treatment.

She was discharged "for insurance reasons" and then she got worse. She told psychiatrists that she was hearing voices and seeing visions about knives. Then Russell found her in the bathroom one day pressing a knife to her throat. He took it away and had her hospitalized. She confessed to one doctor that she was afraid she might hurt someone. On the antipsychotic drug Haldol, she improved slightly.

When Andrea's father died a few months later, she stopped functioning. She wouldn't feed the baby, she became malnourished, and she drifted into a private world. Russell forced her into treatment under psychiatrist Mohammed Saeed. He had not heard from Russell—who claimed not to know—about the hallucinations, and he observed no psychosis himself, so he felt Haldol was unnecessary. After ten days, he discharged Andrea into her husband's care.

Russell was worried, but Saeed assured him that Andrea did not need shock treatment or Haldol. He reportedly told Andrea to "think positive thoughts" and to see a psychologist. However, he did warn Russell that she should not be left alone.

Andrea sat at home in a near-catatonic state. However, on the morning of June 20, 2001, Russell thought it would be okay to leave her with the children for an hour. He was wrong. Once he'd left, Andrea began to fill the tub. She started with Paul, the 3-year-old, holding him underwater until he stopped struggling. Then came Luke, then John and little Mary, and the last one was Noah.

It was no sudden act; Andrea admitted later that she'd been considering it for several months. At times, she indicated that she'd done it because she was not a good mother, and at other times because the children were not developing normally and she had to save their souls while they were still young.

She was charged with knowingly and intentionally causing the deaths of the children with a deadly weapon (water), and her case became a high-profile arena for the battle of medical experts. At her hearing, her prison psychologist, Dr. Gerald Harris, claimed that she wanted to be executed so that she and Satan, who possessed her, would be destroyed. While she pleaded not guilty by reason of insanity, her competency even to be tried came under question. She claimed that Satan was coming to her in prison and conversing with her and she insisted she would not enter a plea of not guilty. She did not need an attorney, and she wanted her hair cut into the shape of a crown. She believed the number of the Antichrist, 666, was imprinted on her scalp. Still, the judge felt she could assist in her own defense.

During the trial in early 2002, which focused on the deaths of Noah, John, and Mary, psychiatrist Phillip Resnick, a specialist in the psychology of parents who kill their children, described the killings as "altruistic." He admitted that Andrea did know that what she was doing was illegal but believed her decision to kill her children was nevertheless right, for the protection of their eternal souls. He believed, after seeing her in her cell on two different occasions, that she suffered from schizophrenia and depression. Contradicting the other doctors, he said each had his own interpretation of the data.

Psychiatrist Park Dietz, for the prosecution, admitted that Andrea was seriously ill, but insisted that she had known that what she was doing was wrong. He also pointed out that she did not act like a mother who believed she was saving her children from Satan, and she had kept her plan a secret from others. She even admitted that she knew what she had done was wrong, and by Texas law these facts were sufficient for the jury to convict Yates of first-degree murder. During the penalty phase, the same jury quickly returned a sentence of life in prison rather than death, and Andrea Yates received this news with little emotion.

While postpartum depression occurs in up to 20 percent of women who have children, psychotic manifestations are rare, and thus much less understood. Only one in five hundred births results in postpartum psychosis, says forensic psychiatric Michael Welner. Unlike in Britain and a few other countries, where the mental health system watches mothers for months afterward for signs of depression and mood swings, people in America have a difficult time understanding how hormonal shifts can actually cause violent hallucinations and ideations concerning their own children. Yet such women can become incoherent, paranoid, irrational, and delusional. They may have outright hallucinations, and are at risk of committing suicide or harming a child—particularly "for the child's own good." The woman herself will not recognize it as an illness.

In Minnesota, Khoua Her, 24, strangled her six children, ages 5 to 11, because she was depressed over her responsibilities. The police had been to her home fifteen times in a year and a half, responding to domestic violence calls, but social workers had not noticed any real danger to the children. The mother had called 911 after the slaughter and spoke of suicide, and she was transported to the hospital with an extension cord still loosely tied around her neck. The children were found scattered around the house. In a plea deal, she received a sentence of fifty years in prison.

Deanna Laney in Texas had decided that she and Andrea Yates were the two witnesses to the world's end, and she believed that God wanted her to sacrifice her three sons as a way for him to work a miracle. So on Mother's Day weekend in 2003, she stoned all three, but her infant survived. Like Yates, she called 911 to turn herself in, and like Yates, she received all kinds of psychiatric testimony at trial, including Dr. Park Dietz for the prosecution. But this time Dietz decided that she was indeed psychotic and did not appreciate the nature of what she was doing. At trial in 2004, a jury found her to be not guilty by reason of insanity and she was committed. There was no evidence in her background up to that time of mental illness or depression.

In America, there are no clear standards in court for how to deal with mental illness in mothers. Such sufferers may have been psychotic and deeply disturbed during a violent episode some time after the birth, but by the time they go to trial, they've usually been restored to better mental health. This makes it difficult for juries, who see them in their improved condition, to believe that these mothers were really suffering that badly.

The way the two sides lined up on the Yates case—she's psychotic versus she's a bad mother—demonstrated the great divide between the concepts of mental illness and legal insanity in the United States.

Dr. Phillip Resnick, on the defense team for both Laney and Yates, said to reporters that some people feel outraged that mothers could kill their own children, while others say that such a crime could only derive from a serious mental illness. Resnick has collected data from over one hundred such cases of both fathers and mothers killing their children, and he finds that juries decide on their emotions and that such emotions favor mothers over fathers in such cases. He attributes the difference to the idea that mothers form a stronger bond with their children and must therefore be ill or overwhelmed to defy it. Juries will also accept testimony about hormonal changes that could trigger violence.

Yates's defense team proved her history of delusional depression, use of antipsychotic drugs, and suicide attempts, and documentation that postpartum mood swings can sometimes evoke psychosis. Yet no matter how many doctors testified to her clear psychological decline, the legal issue hinged on only her mental state at the time of the offense. In other words, as Yates drowned her children one by one, even chasing down 7-year-old Noah to drag him to the tub, did she have any awareness that what she was doing was wrong? If so, then awareness implies the ability to choose.

Since Andrea Yates ignored advice against having more children, waited that morning for her husband to leave, knew that murder was a sin, expected to be punished, and called 911, it appeared that she could control her behavior. Yet that argument depends on a simplistic idea about the relationship between awareness and choice.

Women can experience significant hormonal shifts that trigger radical mood swings. After they've given birth, they may feel depressed, fatigued, and overwhelmed, but the message they receive is that they are supposed to feel elated and joyful. Yates's depression could have been building for a long time without being obvious (although clearly it was obvious), and in *Time* magazine Dallas psychologist Ann Dunnewold indicated that such depressions can evolve into hallucinatory psychosis. Yates certainly reported hallucinations, as well as all the symptoms of extreme depression. Yet the jury apparently did not believe that this had clouded her judgment.

IN THE WAY

Not all family killers are related to the victims. David William Shearing stalked six members of the Robert Johnson family in August 1982 in a park where they were camping in British Columbia, Canada. The case was fully documented in *The Seventh Shadow,* a book by retired sergeant Mike Eastham, the Mountie who investigated it for two years. Shearing shot the adults—Robert and Jackie Johnson and Jackie's parents—and kidnapped the two girls, 11 and 13, using them for his sexual pleasure for several days. He then killed them and put them into the Johnson car with the other four bodies and set it on fire. A complete stranger had murdered three generations of a family.

The Johnsons had been scheduled to be away for two weeks, so no one missed them for a while. Then, when Bob Johnson did not show up for work, friends began to worry. The police searched the rugged Wells Gray Park but found no sign of them. Then a mushroom picker reported a burned-out vehicle of the right description, and police found four burned bodies. They had been shot in the head with a .22. In the trunk they found the girls' burned remains.

The manhunt lasted two years, eventually focusing on a local man who had been in trouble with the law and who knew the park quite well: David Shearing. Under questioning, he finally confessed. He had shot them all and had looted the camper. He reenacted the crime for police and was sentenced to six concurrent life terms.

Despite the title of this chapter, mass murders are not easy to fit into categories. Each of the cases described above has qualities that set it apart from the others, from psychosis to greed, to narcissism, to flagrant aggression. The same can be said of incidents of workplace violence.

CHAPTER 7

Going Postal:
The Disgruntled Employee

ACTING OUT

Each year, several hundred people become victims in mass murders, most often family massacres or through incidents of workplace violence. Often the victims knew their killer, but some only peripherally. Over the decades, the incidents have increased.

While many experts pinpoint the start of workplace violence as the 1980s, in fact it was 1967. That year, Leo Held saw his wife off to work and his four kids off to school on October 24, then drove to the Hammermill Paper Company. An employee there for over two decades, he entered with a .38 revolver, a .45 magnum, and an attitude, shooting three supervisors and two lab technicians. From there he drove to Lock Haven airport and seriously wounded a neighbor who worked there—a woman whom he believed had maligned him. Then he went to the home of Floyd Quiggle, another neighbor, and broke in. He shot Quiggle, killing him, and shot his wife, wounding her. Going to his own home across the street, he locked himself inside and the house was quickly surrounded by police.

Held tried to escape out the back but was shot and wounded. He died at the hospital, leaving behind a mystery as to why he had decided to go on this sudden rampage that had left six people dead. After piecing a narrative together, investigators believed that he was simply angry over missed promotions and other injustices he had imagined he suffered at the hands of bosses and neighbors. Just before he died, he told a nurse he still had "unfinished business"—there had been one more intended victim that he had not yet killed. That person's identity was never revealed.

Nine years later in July 1976, a janitor, Edward C. Allaway, 37, went on a shooting rampage at a library in Fullerton, California, killing seven people. He had decided that his coworkers had been instrumental in the breakup of his third marriage. He was judged to be insane, and thereby escaped incarceration in prison. He was committed instead to Atascadero State Hospital.

The following year, 1977, on Valentine's Day, weight-lifter Frederick Cowan, 33, shot ten people at his workplace in New Rochelle, New York, before killing himself, supposedly because he worshipped Hitler and hated blacks and Jews, and his supervisor was Jewish. Six of his victims died, including a police officer. His intended target, Supervisor Bing, had hidden himself and escaped. Before dying, Cowan had called the police to order lunch and to apologize for the "inconvenience" that he had caused.

Then nearly a decade passed before postal workers started an inexplicable contagion of massacres.

POST OFFICE VIOLENCE

In Edmond, Oklahoma, part-time postal worker Patrick Sherrill, 44, wanted vengeance. On August 19, 1986, two supervisors had dressed him down for poor performance on the job. He had been working as a letter carrier for sixteen months, and according to them had been unable to show professionalism. Once he had been rude to a customer and another time he simply had failed to do what he was paid to do. Clearly, he was not one of those mailmen who would get through sleet or snow to make sure people received their mail.

A loner who had no real community support and no family, Sherrill had been seen peeping at neighbors through a telescope. He was unable to keep a job for very long.

On August 20, he went to work with two borrowed pistols and one hundred rounds of ammunition. At 7:00 A.M., he locked the doors to the post office behind him and went into the room where other employees were busy sorting letters. Although he was gunning for his supervisors, one boss's desk was empty, so Sherrill decided to look for the other one. With a .45, he shot the man and killed him. He then opened fire on the others nearby, walking through the room and shooting anyone he saw. Some people ran but others had no idea what was happening. After ten minutes, with fourteen people dead and six wounded, Sherrill returned to the supervisor's desk, sat in the chair, and put one of his guns to his head to kill himself.

An ex-marine with no real friends, he may have been facing the ultimate failure: loss of his job. The night before the massacre, he had told a friend not to go to work.

This incident was the first of many strikes against postal workers in years to come, which eventually led to someone coining the phrase "going postal"—in other words, snapping and going on a rampage.

Over the course of ten years there were almost thirty killings at U.S. Post Offices, resulting in fifty-four deaths. Among the shooters was mail clerk Joseph Harris. He had threatened his supervisor at his post office in Ridgewood, New Jersey, and when he failed to agree to undergo a fitness-for-duty examination, he subsequently lost his job. He left, and when he did not immediately return, people relaxed. Harris had been a frightening figure, kicking bags of mail and acting as if he was some sort of kung fu expert. Reportedly, he did not like anyone, male or female.

Months went by, and then a year. Most of those who had worked with Harris over the decade he had been at the post office had forgotten about him. But Harris, now 35, had not forgotten his humiliation. He nursed the grudge, letting it build for eighteen months. When he finally decided to act, he gathered his weapons: an Uzi assault rifle, a .22-caliber machine gun with a silencer, hand grenades, knives, a sword, and material to make bombs. Dressing as a Ninja warrior in a black silk hood, black fatigues, and a bulletproof vest, he set the assault for the night of October 9, 1991.

It began when Harris entered the home of his former supervisor. He shot and killed her fiancé and fatally stabbed her with his knife. He also used his samurai sword on her. Then he went to the post office, where he had previously worked on the night shift. He shot two mail handlers, while a driver who saw what was happening rushed off to alert the police. Harris locked himself into a restroom for four hours and finally surrendered to a SWAT team.

Apparently, his intention had been suicide, because he had left behind a two-page suicide note in the room he rented, and in the note he had cited Sherrill as a role model. Harris approved of Sherrill's massacre as the right thing to do. He was charged with and convicted of murder, attempted murder, and unlawful possession of several different weapons.

Thomas McIlvane, another former marine and a fearsome kick boxer who scared people, did the same thing. He wanted to be reinstated in his job at the Royal Oak post office in Michigan and he threatened that if this did not occur, he would outdo the massacre in Edmond. His former coworkers nervously awaited the day when he would show up as other postal workers had done around the country, armed and ready. They felt certain it would happen and had even requested extra security.

When it became known that McIlvane would not be reinstated, supervisors asked headquarters for protection but reportedly received a negative reply. One brave soul phoned McIlvane on November 13, 1991, about five weeks after the news had died down about Joseph Harris's New Jersey assault. As predicted, McIlvane came straightaway with a sawed-off rifle to hunt down those he deemed responsible for getting him fired. For ten minutes, he walked around looking for the "snakes." He killed four people before he then turned the gun on himself.

In 1993, two workers attacked on the same day in Michigan and California. The post office had to start looking for red flags in those they hired: single, white, middle-aged males with a record of assault, mental illness, or problems with authority. Those with a facility with guns and a military record were also scrutinized. Yet the people who were conducting the threat assessments realized that singling out such individuals could trigger their rage or paranoia. Firing them would be the wrong move.

Around the country, forensic professionals began forming organizations to offer risk management and threat assessment assistance, helping employers to see the red flags early and to learn how to avoid the violence. Less threatening means of helping potentially violent workers to either adapt to the job or accept termination were devised. In addition, people who worked at these facilities were educated about their actual level of risk.

A report based on a survey of 12,000 postal employees and 3,000 employees at other jobs, published in 2000, examined just how dangerous the post office could be as a work environment. Known as the Califano Report, it presented certain facts that attempted to defuse the myths about "going postal."

Workers at private postal agencies were at more risk than federal employees, the study concluded. While one in twenty employees were physically assaulted on the job, the risk for postal workers was equal to the risk for others in corporate settings. Fourteen percent of postal workers reported harassment, just short of the sixteen percent average for other jobs. Verbal abuse was higher for postal worker complaints, with over one-third of the work force acknowledging it. They were not more likely than workers at other jobs to become the victims of fatal violence, and in fact their risk was much lower than in some occupations, such as convenience store clerks or cab drivers.

Yet it's not just the post office to which such killers return. Along with the epidemic of post office killings, workplace violence increased dramatically. While such violence can be committed by disgruntled customers (a student delayed in getting a degree) or by people who have no relationship to a company whatsoever (a person who targets a company for symbolic reasons), it tends to be committed by someone who has a work record at the establishment.

The generally stated motive is revenge against someone for doing the killer a wrong. Killers in this context blame others and feel such a degree of anger and frustration that they finally just explode—although this generally occurs as the result of planning, preparation, and mental rehearsal, rather than "snapping." If they cannot find the person responsible, they may act out against anyone close at hand. While it may seem as if they are undermining what they want to gain, in fact they are gaining psychological satisfaction, already nursed via threats and private fantasies.

The *New York Times* ran a study by four prominent journalists of one hundred incidents of rampage killings over the past half century, many of which involved workplace violence. They found that such killers were generally older, educated, experienced with firearms, and often unemployed or at a perceived risk of becoming unemployed. Most had no criminal records prior to the incident, although they may have had a history of problems with authority or rules. More than half had a history of serious mental illness (sometimes undiagnosed), and 56 percent acquired their weapons legally. Many had made specific threats beforehand, but were ignored. They often blamed others for their problems and complained about workplace conditions. Fourteen percent were aware of others who had done a similar act and some wanted to copy or outdo what that person had done. In most cases, clear warning signs had been dismissed or ignored, especially outside stressors from other situations, and most often these were overlooked by family members. One-third of the killers were suicidal, dying at the scene either by outright suicide or by putting themselves into the position of being shot. A few who gave themselves up had initially expected to die.

The *New York Times* journalists had also gone through FBI reports since 1976 about homicide to determine if these massacres had become more common in recent decades. They found that most multiple homicides did not involve four or more victims (and thus did not make most of the lists for mass murders). In fact, rampage killings accounted for about one-tenth of one percent of homicides—much fewer than most people who pay attention to the evening news would probably believe. Yet even so, in the 1990s there was an increase in these incidents. During the 1970s and 1980s they averaged about twenty-three per year, but after 1990 the number increased to thirty-four.

Experts insist that despite appearances, most killers don't arrive at the decision to commit murder at the workplace spontaneously. In fact, their violence tends to develop over time. They fixate and then fertilize their anger at some target. It seems to many of these killers as if their lives are over and they decide that they might as well take some others with them, especially anyone whom they believe caused them to be in the painful state in which they find themselves. Life just has not been fair and they want someone to pay for what has happened to them. Often, they possess the means to make that happen—especially since they believe they have nothing to lose.

In 1997 the National Institute for Occupational Safety indicated that males were three timers more likely to become victims of workplace homicide than females, and that homicide was the second leading cause of death on the job, after car accidents.

While workplace violence has increased, the profile among these killers remains fairly stable, as characterized in the following cases.

ON THE JOB

Joseph Wesbecker had given twenty good years as a pressman to Standard Gravure Printing Company in Louisville, Kentucky, when his supervisors placed him on a long-term disability leave for psychiatric problems from depression. He was 47 and saw no way to get other employment. He had believed that he had a job for life and now he had nothing. He convinced himself that the company had not treated him well. Given his problems, he had requested a less stressful position and instead had been laid off. Around the same time, his marriage had failed and he had incurred heavy losses from investing. Added up, this meant to him that he really had nothing to lose. He began to collect his arsenal.

On Thursday, September 14, 1989, Wesbecker armed himself with an AK-47, an assault pistol, two semiautomatic Mac-11 pistols (just purchased), a .38 revolver, a bayonet, and hundreds of rounds of ammunition. Then he went to the company, where no one had seen him for half a year, took the elevator to the business offices on the third floor, and upon emerging began to shoot whoever was there. As he walked through the hallways, he fired at random. Someone called the police to report the rampage and they arrived in moments, but not before the shooter had done his work.

Wesbecker continued around the building, going down even to the basement to find victims. As some experts later commented, he was trying to annihilate the company, and anyone who was in the building that day represented the company to him. Once he had exhausted his anger, he used a pistol to shoot himself in the face. In about twenty minutes, he had shot twenty-two people in all, and seven of them died.

A psychiatrist whom Wesbecker had been seeing indicated that he suffered from bipolar disorder. Several relatives of the victims sued the makers of Prozac, which Wesbecker had been taking, but no one could prove that the drug itself had caused the crime, so the suits came to nothing.

Wesbecker had made clear threats and given signals that he might do something violent. He had even mentioned hiring someone to do it for him. Workers knew that he had made a list of people he had wanted to kill, but they believed that he had just been venting. Indeed, he had been bent on wiping out a company.

After him came James Pough's suicidal 1990 shooting spree in Jacksonville, Florida, at a General Motors Acceptance Corps. Pough killed ten and wounded four over a petty grievance: General Motors had repossessed his car. Gian Luigi Ferri killed eight people in a San Francisco law office in 1993 before killing himself. That same year, Alan Winterbourne killed three and wounded four workers in an unemployment office. When he killed a police officer, he essentially committed suicide by cop. Tuan Nguyen, who had recently been fired, shot three people at his place of employment, and a year later James Simpson, unemployed, killed five people and himself in Texas. Willie Woods shot four supervisors to death in Los Angeles in 1995, and firefighter Kenneth Thomas did the same in Mississippi a year later.

The list goes on and on, each year producing one, two, or three such workplace massacres, from car washes to employment agencies to manufacturing plants. Like Wesbecker, some killers target the company and its representatives, but others target specific individuals, such as happened quite unexpectedly in Hawaii.

Up to that point, Hawaii had the lowest murder rate in the nation and the Xerox Corporation had known fifty years free of such incidents. All of that changed on November 2, 1999. Byran Koji Uyesugi, 44, was said to be a reclusive man who lived alone, but on that morning he went on a shooting rampage against his coworkers at an office building of the Xerox Corporation on Nimitz Highway. By the time he was done, he had killed seven men in a second-floor conference room with a 9-mm Glock semiautomatic pistol. One victim was his supervisor. He also shot unsuccessfully at an eighth person and when the incident was analyzed later, it appeared that he had targeted people from his own work team. After he was finished, he waved good-bye and fled the scene in a company van. Witnesses reported that he was smiling, as if enjoying his day.

He ended up in a nature preserve, where someone who matched his van to news reports called the police.

They surrounded him as he was sitting in the van, and he held them off for five hours until Uyesugi's brother persuaded him to surrender. At 2:25 P.M. he was arrested. In his home, eleven handguns, five rifles, and two shotguns were confiscated. More weapons were found later, bringing the total to twenty-four, plus the handgun, although he had permits for only seventeen. Twenty 9-mm casings were recovered from the scene.

It was the worst mass murder in Hawaii's history. Uyesugi was charged with first-degree murder and held on a $7 million bail at the Oahu Correctional Centre in Honolulu.

In news interviews, Uyesugi's father admitted that his son had problems with anger and had been ordered to seek counseling for it. Uyesugi seemed to have a low stress threshold, and when he felt pressured, he threatened others, destroyed property, or acted out physically in other ways.

He went to trial in 2000. His defense team did not dispute that he was the gunman, but they argued a defense of mental incapacity. He had schizophrenia at the time of the shooting and was thus unable to judge the nature of his actions. He had allegedly suffered from the delusion that one of his coworkers was an FBI agent and part of a conspiracy that had targeted him, so the trial centered on his state of mind at the time of the shooting, relying on psychiatric experts for both sides.

Uyesugi had been employed for fifteen years at this company as a machine repairman. Neighbors described him as studious and hardworking. Yet he had a history of problems: he had erupted in anger once before on the job. A former Xerox worker, Clyde Nitta, testified that Uyesugi had once gotten upset with some coworkers in 1995 and was reported to have said, "I'll take care of them. I'll shoot all of them." Several people were warned, including two of the men who had died in the shooting. Another worker said that he recalled Uyesugi saying that if he ever got fired, he would shoot as many people as he could. People knew that he had a gun collection and had been on the shooting team in high school, so they had taken his threats seriously.

The prosecution's psychiatrist, Dr. Michael Welner from the Forensic Panel in Manhattan, researched the case, which included talking with the shooter, visiting the crime scene, talking to witnesses, and learning what he could from the defendant's family. He accepted the diagnosis of schizophrenia but concluded that Uyesugi's illness had not prevented him from understanding the illegal nature of his crime. He had acted in a deliberate way, had hidden himself to make the plan work, had demonstrated a long-standing animosity against his coworkers, and had acted in a way that exhibited clear reasoning and intent. When Dr. Welner assessed the man, he found no evidence of hallucinations or disorganization in his thinking. "His actions," he was quoted in the papers as saying, "had to do with his relationship with his co-workers."[1]

It came out that Uyesugi had been under the impression that he was going to be fired, because there were complaints that he was hostile to coworkers and alienated customers. Even his work performance was sub-par. It seemed to the prosecution team that he had believed that he needed to act preemptively. He was going to get those who wanted to be rid of him before they could get him.

The jury found Uyesugi guilty of first-degree murder, and he was sentenced to life in prison without parole. He was also ordered to pay restitution in the amount of $70,000 to the families of the men he had killed.

A BAD TRADING DAY

Workplace mass murderers may also be customers of a company, and become so enraged at something for which they blame the company, they take it out on the employees. The following account was reported in the *Atlanta Journal-Constitution* and the *New York Times*.

During the 1990s, because the stock market seemed to be on an un-ending rise, day trading became a common practice for those people who were seeking easy money that could be made quickly. They would buy in the morning, watch the stock prices rise, and then sell off, pocketing the profits. Some companies even set up high-speed terminals on which people could manage their own accounts, which for some became addictive. It was a gamble and people did lose, but there were stories circulating about how some traders had scored quite impressively and had become rich.

Mark O. Barton was a securities day trader. He had left his job as a chemist to pursue this fast-paced, high-risk lifestyle. No one at the companies where he did business knew that six years earlier he had been the chief suspect in the 1993 hacking deaths of his former wife and mother-in-law, though due to lack of evidence he was never charged. He had purchased a substantial life insurance policy on his wife shortly before she died that had paid $600,000, and he had been having an affair (known to his wife) with a woman named Leigh Ann, who moved in with him after the deaths and eventually became his second wife.

In securities trading, Barton had lost so much of the insurance money during the summer of 1999 that his accounts at two different brokerages had been cut off and he was actually deep in debt. When he had tried reopening one account with a check, it had bounced, so he had made an appointment for Thursday, July 29, to see a manager to restore his trading privileges.

On that afternoon, Barton went to the Buckland business district near Atlanta, Georgia, where the offices for Momentum Securities were located in the Piedmont Center. He had two weapons with him, a Colt .45 and a 9-mm semiautomatic pistol. By some accounts, after entering the brokerage he first made small talk with company employees, waiting for the tardy manager, and by other accounts he simply walked in and started firing. In either case, he allegedly said, "It's a bad trading day and it's about to get worse." Four people died and many were wounded.

Even as police scrambled to respond, Barton left that building, crossed the street, and entered the offices for All-Tech Investment Group, located in Two Securities Center. No one there knew what had just occurred not far from them, and Barton greeted the receptionist in a friendly manner. He then went to the manager's office and began shooting. He next walked out to the main trading floor and aimed at every person he saw. He managed to kill five more and injure many others. Then he escaped.

The police knew who they were looking for, but he had managed to elude them. Going to his apartment, they found the bodies of his family, all bludgeoned to death with a hammer. The two children lay side-by-side in their beds, one with a videogame and one with a teddy bear. Notes implored whoever found them to take care of them. They appeared to have been bathed before being placed in bed. Barton left another note to the effect that his wife was in the master bedroom, and that despite how it looked, he was not responsible for the 1993 killings. He blamed Leigh Ann for his demise, and she was found in the closet with a note in which Barton had pledged his love forever. She had been killed some time before the children.

After the massacre, Barton had taken off in his van, which citizens had spotted and reported, and five hours later the police surrounded him at a gas station. Before they could grab him, he used both of his weapons to shoot himself in the head. Barton's death toll that day was twelve, plus himself. He had wounded twenty-two (the *Times* account says twelve). It was the largest mass murder in Atlanta's history.

While workplace violence is on the rise, most likely with the increase in stress associated with employment rates, negative economic conditions, and other career pressures, no such incident compares to the degree of violence against others when the motives are political or religious. Next we turn to massacres on an ideological scale, fueled by those in power who believe that their philosophies are served only with death.

CHAPTER 8

Visionary Mass Murder: Religion and Politics

Without even considering genocide, many massacres are triggered by political or religious ideas, and at times the two movements ride together behind the same engine. Beginning with those that appeared overtly political, we'll shade into those more clearly centered in violence in the name of religion, with a continuation into the following chapter, which concerns believers within either arena who inspire violent disciples.

A FEMALE CONSPIRACY

In Montreal, Canada, in 1989, Marc Lépine committed the worst massacre in that country's history. When his reasons for it emerged, his delusional disorder was apparent but its particular twist was unique. The massacre and its aftermath were documented in the Montreal paper *The Gazette*.

It was December 6 when Lépine, 25, went to the École Polytechnique, the engineering school at the University of Montreal, to make his political statement and exact his revenge for a lifetime filled with anger, pain, and failure.

Beaten by his father, he nevertheless followed in his father's footsteps in developing a view of women as servile and second class. Psychologically speaking, he was not built for a world in which women were getting educated, acquiring opportunities, and becoming strong and independent. In his mind, they had a place and they should stay there. He began to feel as if women were pushing him out of his own rightful opportunities. Someone, he believed, had to teach them a lesson, and he decided that it would be him.

His plan took months of preparation, but his long-standing hatred held him to it. Finally he chose just the right gun, a Ruger semiautomatic Mini-14 .223-caliber rifle. He told the clerk at the store where he bought it that he was going after "small game." He also purchased a banana clip loadable to thirty rounds and several boxes of ammunition.

He then returned to his apartment. Neighbors knew of him and thought him eccentric and strange, but no one had seen the signs of violence about to erupt.

Weapons gave Lépine a feeling of confidence and power, and he had hoped to enlist in the armed services, but when they refused him they disabled his military ambitions. However, through his readings he had become acquainted with the tale of Corporal Denis Lortie, who in 1984 had stolen military weapons and gone on a rampage, killing three government employees and wounding thirteen. It's possible that he drew inspiration from that incident.

Lépine had a difficult time with employment as well, and in 1986 had been rejected by the École Polytechnique. Life probably looked pretty bleak. Although he had quit one job, he apparently told people that a woman had fired him and that a woman had also replaced him. Both accounts were untrue, but what was true was that he had proved himself a difficult employee wherever he went. He disliked authority and was considered to be rude, obnoxious, and disruptive.

Lépine let his financial resources run out, not bothering to even look for a job, because he knew well in advance that he would no longer need money. He was ready to die and one day wrote a lengthy letter to that effect—his would be a political death, a sacrifice in the name of killing as many feminists as he could, to show other women their place.

"Because I decided to send *Ad Patres* [to the fathers] the feminists who have always ruined my life," he jotted in this letter. "For seven years my life has brought me no joy, and being utterly weary of the world, I have decided to stop those shrews dead in their tracks."[1] He put this note into a jacket pocket and left in a rented car to complete his mission. It came out later that he had made a list of nineteen women mentioned in newspapers, from police officers to politicians, but had decided that he had no time to execute them all.

Lépine had shaved his head in preparation and dressed in a shirt that featured a skull design. He had strapped on a hunting knife and grabbed his new rifle. His target was the École Polytechnique.

When he arrived that afternoon, he sat around for a while on a bench; at a few minutes after 5:00 P.M. he went directly to a classroom in which sixty students had gathered for a lecture. Inside, he ordered the students to separate into male and female groups. They thought it was a joke until he fired a warning shot. He told the men to leave, and they did so while he cornered the ten women. He then explained his reason for being there before he methodically shot them from left to right, killing six. The men waiting outside could hardly believe what was happening.

Striding past them and through the halls, Lépine shot at people as he went, especially women, and took the stairs down to the first-floor cafeteria. Diners who had been urged to leave by fleeing students had dismissed the warnings as pranks. They were all shot, and several died. Those who survived recalled how the madman was smiling the whole time he was shooting, "like he was having a good time."

Lépine went to the third floor via a broken escalator, where he shot a woman, entered another classroom, and killed more female students there. When one wounded young woman near him begged for help, he sat next to her and plunged his hunting knife three times into her chest. Then, apparently emotionally spent after his twenty-minute rampage, he used the rifle to kill himself. His last words were, "Ah, shit."

In all Lépine had killed fourteen women and wounded fifteen students of mixed gender. Yet there were more victims as well. One young man who had escaped hanged himself the following year. In despair, his parents both committed suicide.

Lépine's stated intention of killing feminists as a political statement, and as a way to scare women back to their traditional roles, shocked both genders around the world. Yet it was not the first hate-inspired massacre. Like others before it and many still to come, it was fueled by the frustration that builds into a hardened anger and a need to blame someone and to make that person or group feel one's own pain.

HATE MASSACRES

Earlier during the same year that Lépine killed so many, 26-year-old drifter Patrick Purdy had taken an AK-47 assault rifle and a 9-mm semi-automatic pistol into the Cleveland Elementary School yard in Stockton, California, killing five and wounding twenty-nine (some sources say thirty-nine). The low death toll was amazing, considering he had gotten off some 130 rounds. By some reports, Purdy apparently had decided that too many Asians were coming into the country, and many of his victims had been Asian. He was also obsessed with war, claiming falsely that he had been in Vietnam. Dressing in military fatigues and aligning himself with various revolutionary causes currently in vogue, he set his car on fire right before he went on his rampage. He did not know any of his victims, but had gone to school in this place as a child. Like Lépine, he committed suicide at the scene. The entire incident had lasted four minutes. Two years earlier, he had been judged a danger to himself and others, but he was nevertheless allowed to resume life outside an institution.

Hate crimes can give a lot of momentum to people intent on "purification." In Italy, Wolfgang Abel and Mario Furlan appeared to have thrived on it. They were school chums from privileged homes, and highly intelligent. They began their criminal career in 1977 by burning a man to death in his car. Then they went to Padua, where they fatally knifed a casino employee and a waiter. They used an axe on a prostitute and a hammer on two priests (one suffered twenty-six blows) before they returned to their initial modus operandi by burning alive a hitchhiker who was sleeping in Verona's city center. A homosexual priest became a victim when they hammered a nail into his forehead. Then they attached a wooden cross to a chisel and pushed this into the man's skull.

At almost every scene, starting in 1980, they left notes, attributed to "Ludwig," which explained the reason for the murders. Apparently these two viewed themselves as the last surviving Nazis, and their victims were among those who had "betrayed the true God"—mostly homosexuals and prostitutes, society's "inferior people." Then in 1984 they decided to up the ante. The "Ludwig band" burned down a building in Milan that housed a cinema that showed pornographic films, and six people died inside. Next they used arson on a discotheque, killing a woman and injuring forty more people. When they moved on to a more crowded dance hall, the discotheque Melamara di Castiglione of the Stivere, they were caught. Had they not been discovered, they might have killed as many as four hundred revelers.

They went to trial at the end of 1986. Furlan's handwriting was matched to one of the Ludwig notes, although he and Abel both denied having anything to do with the "Ludwig" killings. In Abel's apartment, a book was found with the name "Ludwig Friar" highlighted. Witnesses had also placed them at the cinema fire and near one of the murdered victims. Twenty-seven charges of murder were leveled against them, but they were found guilty of only ten. Because they were deemed partially insane, both got a sentence of thirty years. However, after serving only three, they were moved into a village and required only to report to the police on a regular basis.

The motives for such murders are generally revenge against imagined crimes, as well as the need to make members of the target race, gender, or religion understand the pain they have "caused." It's payback and a warning, as well as a way for the perpetrator to convince himself that his "sacrifice" might restore the world to its rightful balance. More personally, it's a reaction of deep-rooted fear.

Racism has a long history in the United States and execution of people who represent a despised race was once common in the South. In 1946 in Georgia, a mob of white men executed two black men and two black women. They shot three times at the hapless victims to ensure that they were dead. The murder angered President Harry S. Truman, who then made civil rights a leading issue on his national agenda. The FBI investigated this mass murder for four months, to no avail, despite having several clear suspects.

In racially divided Birmingham, Alabama, on September 15, 1963, a group of men involved in the Ku Klux Klan (KKK) bombed the all-black Sixteenth Street Baptist Church. It was no surprise, since city officials had long practiced oppressive tactics against blacks, using vicious dogs and powerful fire hoses on them, as well as unwarranted imprisonment. Yet inside the church four young girls were preparing for the 11:00 service. Denise McNair, 11, Cynthia Wesley, 14, Carole Robertson, 14, and Addie Mae Collins, 14, were killed in the explosion, and many others were injured. The church was selected because it was known as the center for many civil rights meetings, and at the end of that terrible day riots had broken out around "Bombingham" and two more teenagers were found dead. The story has been retold in a movie, *Sins of the Father,* and in an HBO documentary, "Four Little Girls."

The FBI opened an investigation against four men, but the apparent absence of evidence and political pressures in Alabama kept the cases out of court. Since J. Edgar Hoover had allied himself with the white officials, and FBI agents were allegedly passing information to the Klan, as described in *Agents of Repression* by Ward Churchill and Jim Vander Wall, one can only wonder at how this investigation was actually pursued. In 1968, Hoover closed the case.

It was reopened during the 1970s under a new attorney general in Alabama. One suspect, KKK member Robert "Dynamite Bob" Chamberliss, was eventually convicted in 1977, five years after Hoover's death, while another, Herman Cash, died in 1994. After the FBI reopened the case in 1995, under pressure from a group of black ministers, a grand jury indicted Thomas Blanton and Bobby Frank Cherry in May 2000 on first-degree murder and "universal mischief" charges, and both surrendered. It took a jury less than three hours in May 2001 to find Blanton, now 62, guilty and to sentence him to life in prison.

Finally, there was only one suspect left: Bobby Frank Cherry, whose son proved a key witness when he contradicted his father's alibi. Five estranged family members also testified that Cherry had boasted about the crime, saying he had lit the bomb's fuse. A jury took seven hours to convict him and send him to prison for the rest of his life. That closed the book on one of the deadliest crimes in the history of the civil rights movement. Cherry, a suspect within days of the incident, denied any wrongdoing.

Political murders are generally sparked by fear and hatred, the bottom line of all prejudice. Some group gets targeted for blame for another person's or group's discomfort and their feeling that control is slipping away. The killers then lash out in an effort to annihilate the threat.

Yet such mass killers are not always from the white class, and are not always bent on eliminating those whom they consider of lesser status. Mark Essex was a young black man, troubled by depression, who had decided that his mission in life was to kill white people. To him, this was a matter of affirming his manhood. As documented in the *Times-Picayune* and Peter Herndon's book *A Terrible Thunder*, on the last day of 1972, after several bouts of racial violence, Essex armed himself, went to the police department, and started shooting. Inadvertently, he killed a black police officer as his first victim. He then hid out in a church, but a week later in January 1973 he ended up at a hotel in New Orleans and shot at a number of white customers there. Setting fires as he ran through the hotel, he ended up on the roof. The police converged en masse to corner him. In all, nine people were killed and twelve wounded by bullets, some of which had ricocheted during an intense shootout by the police that also annihilated Essex. On the ground outside, a crowd of blacks was urging him on as a hero, shouting, "Kill the pigs!" Since Essex had given away all his possessions prior to the massacre, it was clear that he'd expected to die in the process—all of this over an obsessive hatred that had finally consumed him.

But sometimes obsession does draw others into a situation in which the only way out is through death.

DEATH AND THE GROUP MIND

On Saturday, November 18, 1978, members of the People's Temple in Jonestown in Guyana, South America, were faced with a dreadful decision. A small party of them had followed Congressman Leo Ryan to the airstrip, killing him along with a reporter, a cameraman, a photographer, and a temple defector. Those people had then raced back to Jonestown to commit suicide with the rest of the followers of Jim Jones.

The grotesque deaths at Jonestown have been documented in numerous books and newspapers, by everyone from cult specialists to journalists for national newspapers, especially the *San Francisco Chronicle*, which lost a photographer in the incident.

The cult members had been more or less prepared for the end. Jones had warned them about the approaching persecution, trained them in how to commit mass suicide, and made its inevitability part of their beliefs. Yet having to answer to it was altogether something else. An official count from the site stood at 909 corpses and no one could say how many had willingly poisoned themselves or were coerced. Some had run into the jungle, but even outside the physical community, a few who were associated with the religion had killed their children and/or themselves. The death toll for the cult from the incident that day, including those at a distance, was around 920. Eighty-five members survived, including escapees and members who just had not been there at the time.

As a young man, Jones had been attracted to the idea of communal living and of being the kind of leader who thought and acted for everyone. He made people believe he could heal them, understand them, and foretell their future. He attracted blacks by saying that he had been a black soul born into a white body and he was there to restore their dignity. In fact, he did offer them a better life than they had in a ghetto. Jones made himself the necessary route to salvation, and he used the fear of imminent catastrophe and signs of persecution to manipulate his followers.

As conditions around them grew tense in the United States, he looked for safe places elsewhere in the world that would protect people in the event of nuclear holocaust and eventually settled his disciples in Guyana. In part, that was to escape hate groups in California, as well as to avoid government investigation. In 1977, over one thousand people followed "Father" to South America to their own version of the Promised Land.

But an organization of relatives and disaffected members, "Concerned Relatives," kept up a campaign of pressure to get authorities to investigate the cult. That kind of activity only inspired Jones to prove to his followers the reality of the battle of good versus evil and to warn them of the approaching Armageddon.

He set up Jonestown as a refuge, but he was unable to keep out those parents who wanted to find and deprogram their children. They portrayed Jones to the press as "evil incarnate," and California newspapers accommodated them with a series of articles documenting Jones's alleged domination of others. A custody battle between parents over a boy who was with his mother in Jonestown triggered the official investigation by Congressman Ryan that resulted in the mass murder/suicide. Lawsuits and criminal complaints, some of which were unfounded, were filed against Jones.

Yet Ryan apparently was satisfied that no one was being coerced to remain in Jonestown. Nevertheless, as he was preparing to leave with sixteen defectors, a man attacked his party with a knife. That hastened their departure to the airstrip, but they were unaware they were being followed and that a "defector" in their midst was actually a plant, placed there to ensure they did not leave.

It seemed that several factors came into play on that fateful day. Jim Jones had become a drug addict and was increasingly disabled by it—to the point where people questioned his leadership and supernatural abilities. Many of the adults who did most of the work were getting tired. People were leaving him and the persecution had reached its apex with the investigational entourage. Jones was clearly feeling as if the dream was eroding and the collective was being corroded both internally and externally.

Since 1976, they had been drilling for the possibility of mass suicide—the "White Night." In other words, Jones was among those leaders who believed that taking his own life demanded the deaths of his followers as part of his proof of ultimate control, so he had prepared them to view themselves as "one" with him and as having no other choice. He even drilled them with beverages that he said were poisoned as a way to "test their loyalty" but also to assure himself of his power over them. What he did could be viewed as a gradual form of mass murder, although the people who laid down their lives that day saw it as the ultimate sacrifice for the ideals of the community.

A member who survived, as documented in Sarah Moran's The Secret World of Cults, indicated that parents fed the cyanide-laced beverage to their children first, killing them before taking their own lives. Some had tried to flee but were forced back at gunpoint by armed guards. Jones himself died by a single shot to the head. Two lawyers who ran off reported that they had heard shots and screams behind them. They returned with the authorities, but it was too late. Due to heat and decomposition as the bodies lay exposed for two days, it was difficult to determine how many may have been outright murdered.

Inevitably, there are some in a cult who are committed to the point of death, while others may be ambivalent. In situations where reports are conflicting, and where a leader has gradually conditioned people to the inevitable, it's difficult to know where to draw the line between voluntary and involuntary death. Certainly those children who had not been able to choose for themselves can be considered victims. The same can be said for the next group of true believers.

RELIGIOUS MARTYRS

Many people have tried to accurately document what happened on February 28, 1993, in Waco, Texas, in the clash between law enforcement and a religious group known as the Branch Davidians, but the truth is elusive. Was their leader, David Koresh, a manipulative psychopath who spotted an opportunity, or was he just a deluded religious leader whose private play was suddenly exposed by inept governmental handling on the world's stage? In other words, it may have been a mass suicide for a cornered prophet who sacrificed people for his own ends, or an unintended massacre by overeager agents who had been chomping at the bit for nearly two months.

HRT sniper Christopher Whitcomb writing in *Cold Zero*, former FBI agent Gregg McCrary in *The Unknown Darkness*, and true crime writer Clifford Linedecker in *Massacre at Waco, Texas* present a chronology of the facts from various angles on that momentous Sunday morning.

More than seventy agents from the Bureau of Alcohol, Tobacco, and Firearms (ATF) moved on a group of wooden buildings known as the Mount Carmel Center outside the southwestern Texas town of Waco. The place was occupied by members of an apocalyptic religious group led by David Koresh. Rumored to be stockpiled inside was an arsenal of explosives and weapons, some of which reportedly had been illegally converted to rapid-fire automatics. That put them under the ATF's jurisdiction.

Linedecker indicates that the local newspaper was running a series of articles about Koresh titled "The Sinful Messiah," based on accounts by defectors like Marc Breault, who later authored *Inside the Cult*. Breault spoke of child abuse and polygamy.

The ATF sent in undercover operatives and then deployed what was supposed to have been a secret attack, though they leaked it to the press—a leak that would find its way into the compound. The Davidians were armed and ready.

At ten o'clock in the morning, three teams formed to enter the building as an agent went to the compound's front door and knocked. Koresh looked out, heard about the warrant, and slammed the door. Then someone—it's not clear who—started shooting. Both sides commenced a fierce gun battle.

Several agents were hit right away. One member of a team that penetrated the building was shot in the head and killed. Several who had climbed to the roof rolled off when hit. From noises inside, said agents in hearings later, it was clear that the cult had some heavy artillery.

Bullets pierced the reporters' cars and then concussion grenades, known as "flash-bangs," exploded among the agents.

ATF bullets pierced the front door, behind which Koresh had been standing. Several people had been hit, including cultists firing from the tower, and four were wounded while five died. The intense skirmish continued for two hours before a truce was called, allowing the ATF to remove their dead and wounded. It turned out that twenty agents had been hit, and four of them died. While the ATF waited through a tense afternoon, they arranged to communicate with Koresh.

Around 5:00, when three cultists walking outside the compound encountered ATF agents, the shooting resumed. Agents killed one and captured one, while the third man got away, and officials then asked Koresh to give up. His response was a scripture reading.

Koresh was not about to give up. According to his millennial beliefs, this was the day for which he and his followers had been waiting and preparing. More than one hundred people accepted Koresh's self-alleged divine gifts and ability to dictate God's wishes. Several apostates who were advising the ATF indicated that a siege could very well trigger a mass suicide.

The ATF was soon reinforced with local police officers, Texas Rangers, members of the FBI's Hostage Rescue Team (HRT), the FBI's Special Agent in Charge from the San Antonio office, a bomb squad, and several U.S. Marshals. Koresh released only four children, ranging in age from three to six, and everyone settled in for a long night.

Breault provides a history of the Branch Davidians as an offshoot of the Seventh-Day Adventist Church. He also details how Koresh rose to power and eventually took over. In the beginning, his name was Vernon J. Howell and he was a high school dropout with the gift of gab. His charismatic manner and prodigious memory won him many followers. Like other Seventh-Day Adventists, he believed that the final battle between good and evil could happen at any time, and when it did, only a select number would witness the return of Jesus Christ and be saved.

Howell affirmed that he was the harbinger out of the Book of Revelation, the one who could interpret the prophecies of the Seven Seals. He divided husbands from wives and claimed the women and girls as his own. He dubbed his male followers Mighty Men and they were to be his primary soldiers. Then he changed his name to David Koresh and prepared his flock for martyrdom. They stockpiled food and collected arms to defend themselves from the "Babylonians." He even taught the children that suicide might one day be required and showed them how to do it with cyanide or a gun.

Throughout the standoff, the FBI's own people were working at odds with each other: negotiators insisted that tactical behavior only fulfilled Koresh's prophecy, while the HRT personnel believed that encroaching on his territory weakened him in the eyes of his followers.

Koresh informed the FBI that he'd been hit by two bullets. He refused medical assistance, but he did release ten more children, including a baby. A psychological consultant was convinced that Koresh himself would never surrender. Negotiations went back and forth for days, with nothing resolved, although Koresh let a few more people out. The FBI got word of a plan that he and his followers would pretend to surrender but instead would start shooting. The FBI began to realize that this man was unpredictable and could be dangerous.

The roots of a violent encounter like this can often be the result of interaction. The group itself would probably not become violent without the catalyst of aggression or persecution. Since such groups are easy targets for "normal" people to demonize, their setup tends to invite a clash. One psychiatrist who came to the command center early, Dr. Park Dietz, read through all the reports and said that Koresh appeared to have antisocial and narcissistic traits, as well as paranoid and grandiose delusions. While some appeal to the rational side of his personality might work short-term, in the long run his psychopathology would erupt. He could become dangerous.

Over the fifty-one days that the siege endured, the revolving teams of negotiators kept trying to resolve things peacefully and save the largest number of people possible. Promises and threats were exchanged, and Koresh practiced several delaying tactics. Just after dawn on Monday morning, April 19, the FBI phoned the compound to warn those inside that they were going to use tear gas. Three minutes later, two combat engineering vehicles approached the buildings, punched holes into the fragile walls, and began to spray gas into the compound.

Abruptly, the Davidians opened fire. Several hours went by as the standoff continued and the FBI pleaded, but just after noon the buildings quickly went up in flames and the fire spread fast. Agents close to the buildings heard gunfire, and they assumed that the people inside had decided on mass suicide.

By the end of that shocking day, eighty-three people had been found dead, twenty-three of them children under 17. Koresh's body was later identified by dental records. He had been shot in the head. Many of the victims had died from gunshot wounds. Over one hundred firearms were eventually recovered from the scene.

Accusations were flung from both sides that the other had started the fire, and the FBI brought to court what it felt was clear evidence that the

Davidians had done it. Agents produced surveillance audiotapes of people inside the compound joking the day before about "catching on fire." On the actual day, there were recorded commands to "spread the fuel" and "light the torch," yet survivors who had escaped claimed there had been no suicide plan.

The subsequent investigation showed that the fire had three points of origin, which would not have happened accidentally. Yet if it was true that tear gas was flammable, then the amount pumped into the compound could easily have caught fire. The question was, what was the true source of the fire? Had the tanks knocked over oil lamps? If so, why hadn't the fire begun earlier? No one seemed to have satisfactory answers.

David Koresh had decided that the Fifth Seal of Chapter 6 in the Book of Revelation predicted that Armageddon would occur there at Mount Carmel. It describes those who were slain for the Word of the Lord and mentions a waiting period, after which the entire community would be killed. According to Koresh's understanding, through this violence, he and his people were to achieve salvation. While some claim that the government was entirely responsible for what happened, due to their inept and unprovoked attack, it's also possible that Koresh realized he was in trouble and had used the opportune moment to "deliver his people" by ensuring their deaths as martyrs.

Whatever the case, others have decided that the government should pay, and this is supposedly what led to the largest massacre on American soil. A man from Decker, Michigan, quietly drove a yellow Ryder rental truck through the streets of Oklahoma City on the morning of August 19, 1995—two years to the day of the tragedy at the Branch Davidian compound in Waco, Texas, that ended the lives of eighty-three people. He parked outside the Alfred P. Murrah government building and walked away. By the time the 4,000-pound bomb exploded at 9:02 A.M., he was blocks away, with earplugs hindering the noise of a huge building collapsing. Then he got into a beat-up car without a license plate and drove away. He considered himself a hero, without a thought for the 168 men, women, and children who were dead or dying, and the more than 500 who would turn up injured. To Timothy McVeigh, the bomber, they were "collateral damage," just the price to be paid for sending the government a dramatic message.

He was caught, tried, and executed, and his actions had the unsettling effect of letting the American people know that terrorists who could strike anytime, anywhere lived among us.

MASSACRE FOR TRANSFORMATION

Morin Heights is a popular ski resort near Montreal in the French-speaking Canadian province of Quebec. On October 4, 1994, a condominium fire attracted the fire brigade, who found two charred bodies. The building was owned by Jo Di Mambro, 69, so officials anticipated that he would be one of the victims and that his friend, Luc Jouret, 47 and a former doctor, could be the other. Di Mambro was the founder of a religious organization known as the Order of the Solar Temple, and Jouret its reputed prophet.

However, the autopsy revealed otherwise: the victims, male and female, had been murdered. Upon closer inspection of the home, three more bodies were found in a closet—a man, woman, and child, dead for several days. They were Tony Dutoit, stabbed fifty times in the back; his wife, Nicki, also stabbed several times in the back, as well as twice in the chest and four times in the throat; and Christopher-Emmanuel, 3 months old, who was stabbed six times in the chest with a wooden stake.

Authorities were stumped, but it wasn't long before their questions became part of an international inquiry. The Dutoits had been members of Di Mambro's Solar Temple sect, and a list found in the chalet indicated that the order had six hundred members. A rumor developed that Di Mambro had sent one of his "knights" to assassinate the Dutoit infant, Christopher-Emmanuel, because he believed the boy to be the Antichrist. A warrant was issued for the arrest of Di Mambro, with Luc Jouret.

The next day, fires broke out across the Atlantic Ocean. In Cheiry, Switzerland, on October 4, a fire burned a farmhouse owned by 73-year-old Albert Giacobino. It was around midnight. Firemen responded and soon found a man was lying on a bed with a plastic bag over his head. The fire appeared to be part of a suicide gesture. It was the farmer, shot in the head.

The police came and soon found several incendiary devices installed around the house. They went into what appeared to be a garage, but once inside saw that it was actually a meeting hall. Eventually they found a secret door. To their astonishment, inside was a room with crimson wall-to-wall carpeting, tall mirrors, and red satin draperies in which lay a number of corpses organized in a circle, like spokes radiating from the hub of a wheel. Their heads outward, they were arranged around a triangular alter. Among scattered champagne bottles, investigators counted eighteen people, many of them wearing what appeared to be white, gold, red, and black ceremonial garments and capes. Many of these people also had plastic bags over their heads, like the man in the house. In an adjacent room they found three more corpses.

There was blood as well, and it soon became clear that most of the people had been shot in the head and ten had been suffocated. A few bodies showed evidence of having been beaten. The investigation concluded with a time-of-death estimate of October 3, the day before.

Then about a hundred miles away, there was a similar discovery in a Swiss skiing village. In Granges-sur-Salvan, a tourist spotted flames at 3:00 A.M. on the morning of October 5. The fire department found three adjacent ski chalets burning. All three had been rigged with gasoline bombs. Inside were numerous victims, including three teenagers and four children. Altogether in two of the three chalets, there were twenty-five badly charred corpses. Many had been shot in the head, some as many as eight times. They were members of the Order of the Solar Temple, as were the twenty-two dead people from the other Swiss village. The order owned the damaged buildings.

In subsequent weeks, after the autopsies, a magistrate determined that of all these deaths, only fifteen had been willing suicides. Many more people had been lured into a ceremony, where they were killed, and seven seemed to have been executed outright. The authorities searched for the cult's leaders.

By the late 1980s, membership in the Solar Temple had reached as high as 600. *Time* reporter Michael Seville wrote that Jouret and Di Mambro had collected as much as $93 million from their followers' assets, selling them and profiting from the proceeds. According to an organization called Religious Tolerance, Luc Jouret had convinced followers that in a previous life he had been a member of the fourteenth-century Christian order the Knights Templar, and that he was now the third incarnation of Christ. According to him, after members left their physical bodies on Earth, via conflagration, they would meet together again via "death voyages" that took them to the star Sirius. In Jouret's doctrine, death was an illusion and life would continue in this other place in a higher form.

As membership declined and rumors of fraud and financial mismanagement plagued the order, preparations were made to finalize the departure plan. As part of Jouret's transformation scheme, he had rigged gasoline bombs at the various suicide sites to go off at the ringing of a phone. Whoever was near the bombs would be incinerated.

During the investigation that linked the three mass death sites, authorities discovered that some of the deceased members had written letters to relatives, officials, scholars, and newspapers to explain what they were about to do. They even admitted to murder, saying that they had executed traitors, but that most of the shootings had been merely a way to help weaker members to make the transition. Only the "awakened" had been able to take their own lives, because they were more spiritually advanced. They all sought a higher realm of spiritual consciousness than was possible to achieve on Earth. The "Masters" had left the planet on March 31, 1993, and January 6, 1994, taking with them the spiritual energy of the seven planets. They had gone to another planet, burning their residences behind them to avoid contamination by the uninitiated. They wanted all the faithful to join them.

Cars belonging to cult members were found at the Chiery train station, abandoned, and a .22 that was linked to the Chiery ritual deaths was found in Granges-sur-Salvan. In seemed that the person who had done the shooting in one place had driven that same night to the other to carry out more killings. Also, the suicide notes, supposedly written before the deaths, had post office dates that indicated they'd been mailed afterward. The shooter was apparently still at large.

Although it was first believed that Di Mambro and Jouret had orchestrated the suicide/slaughter and then gone to hide out until they could emerge and spend the money they had fleeced, their bodies were soon identified as being among the Swiss dead. Either they had bought into their spiritual philosophies or they had decided to evade evident trouble.

Despite Jouret's charisma, people in the commune resented his controlling manner, so they voted him out as Grand Master, which caused a rift in the European community and angered Di Mambro. He began to think less of his chosen protégé. As well, Di Mambro had left a letter deploring the manner of the deaths at Chiery, saying they were nothing but carnage perpetrated by the incompetent Jouret.

As reporters uncovered Jouret's past, they learned that prior to his involvement with the Solar Temple, he had been part of a racist, neo-Nazi magical society, cofounded by former Gestapo officer Julien Origas. He'd made a grab for power and lost, so he left. In the Solar Temple, he'd made the same lunge for power, and here, too, he had failed.

It wasn't long before the more worldly reasons for the order's grisly exit emerged. Apparently during the elaborate rituals for communal enlightenment, Di Mambro liked to use laser tricks to make the Holy Grail and the spiritual "Masters" appear to believers, but one of his assistants had grown disgusted and divulged the secret. That man was Tony Dutoit, one of the murder victims in Canada, who had been stabbed fifty times.

Also, other pressures were closing in. First, Di Mambro had diabetes, kidney failure, and incontinence, and believed he had cancer. He was also being investigated for money laundering. Worse were the spiritual affronts. Di Mambro had wanted to create an order of cosmic children, including his own daughter, but at the age of 12, Emmanuelle was rebelling. She no longer wanted the "purity" of forbidden contact; she wanted to be among kids her own age. In addition, Di Mambro's son, Elie, had discovered Di Mambro's trickery and had denounced his father to many members, who then demanded the return of their funds.

In addition to significant internal rifts, the order was having problems with the culture at large. In 1991 a defecting member began to spread word in Quebec that the Solar Temple was dangerous. She urged others to do the same, which sparked a number of lawsuits against the order. Two years later, the Solar Temple came under police surveillance for possible connections with a political assassin organization, and then Jouret was pulled into a scandal involving illegal arms.

At the same time, the fifty-one-day siege had begun in Waco, Texas, and there was a lot of bad press against cults, which inspired more defections. The Solar Temple doctrines suddenly indicated that the stage of consciousness that could evolve on Earth was at its climax, and it was time to move on.

Over a year after the first series of mass suicides, on December 15, 1995, in a forested area near Grenoble, France, known as the Well of Hell, sixteen people were found dead and burned. Fourteen were arranged in a wheel-like pattern, heads outward, which came to be regarded as a star. This night was chosen for its association with the winter solstice, and all of the dead were members of the Solar Temple. Three were children, and there was evidence that not all of the victims had willingly gone to their deaths. One woman's jaw was fractured, as if she had struggled. Most had drugs in their system that had induced lethargy and sleep, and four people had left behind suicide notes. They hinted at another mass suicide to follow. Two bodies that lay not far away were a police officer and an immigration inspector. Reconstruction of the incident indicated that they were the shooters and had started the fire.

The police monitored known members of the order throughout 1996, during the solstice and equinox seasons, but when nothing happened they eased their vigilance. Yet it wasn't over. On March 22, 1997, another mass suicide in St. Casimir, Quebec, brought the total deaths for this religious cult to seventy-four. This one had nearly been averted. Five adult members and three teenagers (two sons and a daughter) had gathered during the spring equinox on March 20. When their incendiary equipment failed, the teenagers persuaded their parents to let them go. Then the adults succeeded at burning down the house and all were killed. Four of them had arranged their bodies in the shape of a cross.

In 1998 the police prevented a German psychologist from carrying out yet another mass suicide. She had gathered twenty-nine people believed to be members of the Solar Temple in the Canary Islands. None of them died.

Piecing the tale together, experts suggest that when Jouret and Di Mambro realized that several governments were preparing for investigations, they translated this as "end times" persecution. Prior to the night of the mass slaughter/suicide in Switzerland, Di Mambro and twelve of his followers had engaged in a "Last Supper" to affirm their spiritual ideals. Then the violence began. In Switzerland, the "awakened" fifteen had killed themselves by poison, while thirty-eight others had been shot. Eight were considered traitors to the order, and were thus executed. The Order of the Solar Temple is now believed to be dormant, if not disbanded altogether.

The mind of the fanatic, according to social philosopher Eric Hoffer in *The True Believer,* needs something to worship, even to the point of annihilation. He will sacrifice everything for the spiritual vision. Cults that promise a higher order from extreme discipline appeal to a certain type of mind, one that is

- frustrated with the way things are,
- confident of the potential for human perfection,
- eager to believe in a single truth,
- able to envision an unprecedented society,
- ready for action, and
- hungry for structure.

Another cult of like-minded members willing to give up everything to their ideals was Heaven's Gate. While not a mass murder like the Oklahoma bombing or even the Solar Temple, in another way, it may be just as diabolical to persuade people to die for a belief when the leader, a human, has decided for his own convenience that it is time.

A peaceful and secretive group, the members of Heaven's Gate made occasional forays into recruitment, but most of their time was spent in rigorous training for reaching a higher plane of consciousness. Religious scholar Catherine Wessinger calls the groups that form around these doctrines millennialists, and in *How the Millennium Comes Violently* she says that they're motivated by an ultimate concern: "the belief in an imminent transition to a collective condition consisting of total well-being, which may be earthly or heavenly."[2]

Salvation is offered to the entire group and it's generally ensured through a charismatic leader who knows how to socialize converts, reinforce beliefs, and keep the group focused. Monastic discipline, special diets, and social withdrawal cultivate dependence on the leaders and encourage the loss of individuality.

Marshall Herff Applewhite, the leader of what would eventually be called Heaven's Gate, was a man who could easily persuade people to accept his ideas and follow. In 1972 he admitted himself into a psychiatric institution over his obsession with sexuality. There he met nurse Bonnie Lu Trousdale Nettles, a member of the Theosophical Society. They discovered a mutual fascination with UFOs and astrology and came to believe that they were the earthly incarnations of ancient aliens: They were the Two Witnesses mentioned in Chapter 11 of the Book of Revelation, placed on this Earth to "harvest souls." Subsequently, they severed ties with family and friends to go spread their message.

What they told people was similar to what many other end-times cult leaders preached: They (the Two) would be persecuted and put to death by their enemies, their bodies would lie in the open for three and a half days, and they would prove their deity by rising from the dead and disappearing into a cloud. From there they would ascend to a higher level to be with God. They believed the biblical "cloud" was actually a spaceship, and they expected to be welcomed aboard. Indeed, this was their only means of salvation from the "Luciferians," who were evil aliens who enslaved humans through worldly concerns like jobs, sex, and families. Those who believed in the message could join the Two and be saved as well.

The Two insisted that to be saved, spiritual-minded individuals must recognize that the appearance that most humans have souls is merely an illusion. Only those who truly had souls and were ready to be harvested by God would recognize the truth.

"We're going to stage, so that it can be witnessed," said Applewhite on a news broadcast, "that when a human has overcome his human-level activities, a chemical change takes place and he goes through a metamorphosis just exactly as a caterpillar does when he quits being a caterpillar and he goes off into a chrysalis and becomes a butterfly."[3]

They managed to accumulate a group of disciples who were willing to leave their families and worldly goods to have the chance for salvation. Then Applewhite and Nettles gave a date for their departure. When nothing happened, they had to persuade their followers that there would be another opportunity. Some left in disgust but many remained to await the next set of instructions. The Two renamed themselves "Do" and "Ti" and went underground with their group, diminished from around two hundred adherents to only eighty.

In 1985, Ti died of cancer and was not physically resurrected. Applewhite had to devise an explanation, so he said that Ti had gone on before them to get things ready. She would pilot the "mothership" that would carry them to a better place. However, it would take a while for her to return. In the meantime, the group got busy.

In 1996 they rented a large seven-bedroom house in the wealthy community of Rancho Santa Fe, north of San Diego, California. There they developed a computer business as Web page designers and renamed themselves Heaven's Gate. At this time, they had only around twenty-five adherents, but through Internet communications they gained more.

Then in November and December of 1996, a comet called Hale-Bopp made a big splash. Its last visit had been in 2200 B.C., viewed then as a harbinger for the arrival of a great peacemaker who would visit civilizations around the world to deliver a sacred doctrine. He would save true believers from the torment of the end times. Do told his followers that Ti had communicated telepathically to him that Hale-Bopp was the sign. She would be in a spaceship on its tail. It was time.

On Friday night, March 21, 1997, the members of Heaven's Gate went to a restaurant where they ordered thirty-nine identical meals of salad and pot pies, and finished off with cheesecake—their final earthly meal. The next day, when the comet was considered closest to Earth, they started the process. Everyone dressed identically in black long-sleeved shirts and black sweat pants, with new black-and-white Nike tennis shoes. On their left shirtsleeves were armband patches on which the words "Heaven's Gate Away Team" were stitched. All of them packed a small overnight bag with clothing, lip balm, and spiral notebooks, and they placed these bags at the foot end of their beds. They also put three quarters and a five-dollar bill into their shirt pockets.

They appeared to later investigators to have worked in three teams. The first team of fifteen received the barbiturate phenobarbital mixed into pudding or applesauce. They then drank vodka to wash it down. A lethal dose was some fifty to one hundred pills. It's surmised that after consuming this toxic mix, they lay on their beds with plastic bags over their heads until they passed out. Those who still lived removed the bags and covered their bodies with purple shrouds. The following day, Sunday, the next team of fifteen followed. Finally there were seven on Monday, and then only two. The "helpers," both women, were not shrouded but had placed plastic bags over their heads.

Deputy Sheriff Robert Bunk went over to the mansion on the afternoon of Wednesday, March 26. An overpowering stench indicated the presence of corpses, so he called for backup. Together, the two officers entered the home and what they found surprised them. Lying on cots were thirty-nine bodies. Among the victims were twenty-one women and eighteen men, all white, from ages 26 to 72. It was the largest mass suicide to date to occur within the United States.

San Diego County medical examiner Brian Blackborne soon announced another disturbing discovery: seven members of the cult had
been castrated, including Applewhite. Former cult members admitted to
reporters that it had been part of "crew-mindedness."

Then there was yet another shock. On March 30, writer Lee Shargel
told David Brinkley on a television talk show that Applewhite had cancer. People who heard this wondered if he had led thirty-eight other
people into taking their lives simply because he did not wish to go alone.
Yet autopsy reports showed no sign of cancer in his body.

It's unlikely that the full story will ever be known of the mystery of
the thirty-nine suicides. Like the Waco and Solar Temple situations, perhaps a leader decided that he had to end it, and that this meant taking
his flock with him. Or perhaps the mass deaths were so entangled in
genuine belief that nothing more nefarious can be blamed beyond a
human response to apocalyptic philosophies.

Yet violence-prone cults don't only turn inward on their own members. Some true believers are sent out to accomplish deadly missions.

CHAPTER 9

Spreading the Damage

MAKING DISCIPLES INTO SLAYERS

Nearly 200 people were killed and over 1,400 injured when ten bombs ripped through Madrid's commuter train system during morning rush hour on March 11, 2004. Spain initially blamed Basque separatists for the bombings, but after police found a van with detonators and an audiotape of quranic verses near where the bombed trains originated, the interior minister said other lines of investigation were opened. The Arabic newspaper *Al-Quds al-Arabi* said it had received a claim of responsibility issued in the name of Al-Qaida.

Since the September 11, 2001, attacks in the United States, Spain has been at the forefront of a vigorous campaign to round up Al-Qaida cells, and over the past several years has detained and convicted a number of operatives. The terrorist movement had used Spain as a staging ground for attacks elsewhere, but the campaign against them made Spain a hostile environment for the Islamist militants.

An e-mailed claim of responsibility, signed by the Brigade of Abu Hafs al-Masri, was received at the Arabic newspaper's London offices and said the brigade's "death squad" had penetrated "one of the pillars of the crusade alliance, Spain." It went on to say that "this is part of settling old accounts with Spain, the crusader, and America's ally in its war against Islam."

Despite domestic opposition, Spain had been a strong supporter of the U.S.-led war on Iraq, which had been going for nearly a year, and many terrorists linked to Al-Qaida had been captured in Spain. After an emergency cabinet meeting, a somber Prime Minister Jose Maria Aznar vowed to hunt down the attackers. "This is mass murder," he said.

The incident in Spain occurred exactly two and one half years after the terrorist attacks against the United States by one of the suspect groups—an attack that had been instrumental in the decision to go to war with Iraq. On the morning of September 11, 2001, nineteen Islamic fanatics boarded four different American passenger jets. At some point during the flights, they took over. Assuring the passengers that everything would be okay, they took over the pilots' seats. In quick succession, two planes crashed into the Twin Towers of New York's World Trade Center (WTC), one flew into the Pentagon in Washington, D.C., and one was aborted in a field over western Pennsylvania, believed to have been aiming toward another symbolic American structure.

More than five thousand people were injured or killed in the day's events, many jumping from floors high up in the WTC in full awareness of what they faced, others feeling the building's pancaking floors come crashing down on top of them. Hundreds died in terror aboard the planes.

The suspected mastermind of these shocking events was Osama bin Laden, a Saudi-born Islamic fundamentalist millionaire operating out of Afghanistan who had long declared his intent to kill Americans with terrorist acts. He was implicated in a failed attempt in 1993 to bomb the WTC, in which six people died and over a thousand were injured, and the trials for those terrorists had just ended in convictions, with sentencing pending. Bin Laden was also implicated in the 1998 attacks on U.S. embassies in Africa. It was his intent to wage a "jihad," or holy war, with the "fatwa," or religious imperative, to eliminate Americans, military or civilian.

He had warned journalists of a "very big one," and many believe in retrospect that he was referring to the September 11 bombings. His stated purpose for these acts was to purify his Muslim land of all nonbelievers, and since history shows that American aggression has often harmed civilians, his intention was to retaliate in kind. To him, it is acceptable to kill any and all Americans. To rouse passion in his followers to do the same, he preaches that this mission is "the duty of every individual Muslim who is able, in any country where this is possible."

While some criminologists believe that this type of event will set off more acts of a similar nature, which will be known collectively as aeronautical mass murder, it's just as likely that this was one of many forms of attack by terrorists. They might use trucks, trains, or any other form of aggression that involves vehicles that can cause massive damage.

Bin Laden is a role model for extremist Islamic militants and he has high praise for followers such as the suicidal hijackers who are willing to be martyrs for the cause. So far, he has rallied thousands to his side who cheered for what took place on September 11. Many have stated their willingness to do his bidding and to die for his holy cause.

Bin Laden is not the first to have created such an atmosphere of obedience and adoration. There have been others.

KILLING FOR TRUTH

On March 20, 1995, five members of the Aum Shinrikyo cult in Tokyo, a cult bonded in violence, went into five different subway stations and boarded trains that were all heading toward a central station near the National Police Agency headquarters. Devoted to "truths" about the creation and destruction of the universe, they did not hesitate to torture and kill people. Their goal that early morning was mass murder. To accomplish this, they placed bags of the nerve agent sarin onto the floors of the trains, punctured them to release the gas, and disembarked. The fumes affected over five thousand commuters and killed twelve. Five days prior to that, this same group had attempted but failed to release botulinus bacteria. Their experiments with poisonous gas a year before—aimed at killing three judges scheduled to hear a lawsuit against them—had injured over six hundred and killed seven. Their agenda was clearly destructive.

Scientists and doctors who were members of the cult had the knowledge and the access to technology to use these weapons of mass destruction, making the religious cult quite lethal. Even worse, members did not have to submit to government demands to inspect their facilities, so they were able to work on their nefarious projects in secret. Cult members were suspected in numerous attacks on defectors and critics, many of whom died. They even had their own hospital in Tokyo where they could administer whatever form of torture or death they pleased. Some of their extreme ascetic practices and initiations even involved killing loyal members. Japanese police surmised that between 1988 and 1995 the cult killed thirty people and inspired two suicides.

After the attack on the subway, the police led a raid against the twenty-five known centers for the religion in Japan, to which the leaders responded with terroristic threats. They even attempted to release hydrogen cyanide into another subway station, but they failed because the device malfunctioned.

During the investigative sweep, more than two hundred Aum practitioners were arrested, including leader Shoko Asahara. He was known to have sold his blood and his dirty bathwater to disciples to allow them to partake of his unique DNA and he had openly urged them to commit violence for him. Asahara was charged with murder and the production of illegal drugs. His various trials dragged out for years, but in February 2004, Asahara was given the death sentence for his part in over two dozen murders. Eleven of his disciples received a similar sentence.

The cult, while much smaller now and stripped of its official recognition as a religion, continues to thrive and has renamed itself Aleph. Proponents are awaiting their version of Judgment Day, when all nonbelievers will be annihilated. Another public attack may yet occur.

What inspires people to participate in such violence, especially educated professionals? Why would scientists be so drawn to it? In *How the Millennium Comes Violently*, Catherine Wessinger indicates that the success of Aum was its appeal to intelligent, successful people who disliked Japanese conformist society. Aum offered enlightenment via mystical experiences and the ability to rise above the masses. Almost half of the ten thousand members in Japan were female and many were young. "It was believed," writes Wessinger, "it was possible to become a superhuman."[1] The personal soul could become more powerful in a collective of such souls, and through these enlightened communities the Earth could be transformed and saved from nuclear annihilation. But all of this would only arrive with attacks on the social status quo. That meant annihilation of unbelievers.

While mass murders are generally thought to be committed by lone individuals, people like Asahara actually spread their venom to others, inspiring them to act out and ensuring the deaths of many more than could one person alone. It seems to require a specific type of leader—one who can inspire others to yield their wills and sense of morality. But history is full of such people, and some of them are clearly psychopathic.

REVOLUTION

On July 31, 1969, two homicide detectives from Los Angeles, California, investigated a lone killing in Malibu. Gary Hinman, a 34-year-old musician, had been stabbed to death. On the wall of his living room was a message written in what turned out to be Hinman's blood: "Political Piggy." A suspect driving Hinman's car, Bobby Beausoliel, had been picked up and there was blood on his clothes. Beausoliel lived on an old movie ranch with a group of hippies led by a man named Charlie, who claimed to be Christ. This man was questioned on August 6.

Three days later, on Saturday, August 9, at the home of film director Roman Polanski, a massacre occurred that would make headlines around the world. Five people were slaughtered in a blood-drenched spree, including Polanski's wife, Sharon Tate, 26, an actress and eight months pregnant at the time.

The first victim apparent to the police was a hapless young man named Steve Parent, 18, who was just in the wrong place at the wrong time, visiting a resident of the guest house. He had been shot four times in his car as he was leaving the premises. Inside the preternaturally quiet home were two blood-covered bodies: Sharon Tate, stabbed sixteen times, had a nylon rope tied loosely around her neck. A long end had been tossed over an overhead rafter and then tied around the neck of hair stylist Jay Sebring, Tate's former beau. He had been shot once and stabbed seven times. On a door, the word "pig" had been written in blood.

And there were victims who apparently had unsuccessfully tried to flee. Outside on the lawn lay Voytek Frykowski, bleeding profusely from his many wounds. He had been shot five times and stabbed fifty-one times as well as struck thirteen times in the head. Nearby was coffee heiress Abigail Folger, stabbed twenty-eight times.

Investigators puzzled over who could have been so angry or vicious or deranged as to mount such an intense attack on so many people at once. At a time when 90 percent of crimes were committed by someone the victim knew, and when most of them were easily interpreted, this frenzy appeared to be an altogether senseless crime. Nothing appeared to have been taken. The word "pig" meant nothing in particular, aside from the way the police were referred to by angry youths in the hippie culture. But these victims had not been police officers. They belonged to the Hollywood set. In fact, the police did have clues, but they did not realize it for several months.

Despite a similar bloody message written on a wall that July in the Gary Hinman homicide, that victim was not immediately associated with this massacre. It was assumed that the five killings at the Polanski residence had been the result of some drug transaction gone awry. Nor was the incident that followed the next night thought to be related. A married couple, Leno and Rosemary LaBianca, had just come home from a trip. Leno was reading the paper in the living room about the shocking murders and Rosemary had prepared for bed when someone entered their home and attacked them. Their adult children discovered them the following day.

Pillowcases had been placed over the heads of both victims and a carving fork was immediately visible sticking out of Leno's abdomen. The killer or killers had crudely carved "War" into his chest and used his blood to write "Death to Pigs," "Rise," and "Healter [sic] Skelter" on the walls. Then they apparently had a snack, helping themselves to food in the kitchen, before leaving. Leno was stabbed twelve times with a knife, which had been left in his throat, and he had fourteen puncture wounds from the fork. Rosemary had been stabbed forty-one times, including some wounds that appeared to be postmortem. The last person to have seen her alive the prior evening recalled how she had worried about the recent attacks at the Polanski residence. She had mentioned that someone had been coming into their home while they were away.

For a while, the police were clueless. They were unable to connect anyone who knew the victims from either massacre to the gruesome deeds. Nor could they determine a clear motive. In fact, the case did not break until they simply got lucky.

In October, a young woman named Susan Atkins spilled the beans while in prison for another crime, gleefully taking credit for her involvement in the massacre. That led the police to her associates, an odd collection of unemployed hippies living on the Spahn ranch outside the city. Eventually they arrested three of the women alleged to have been involved, Susan Atkins, Leslie Van Houten, and Patricia Krenwinkel, along with Charles Manson, their supposed leader, and a drifter called "Tex." During the investigation, documented by prosecutor Vincent Bugliosi in his book *Helter Skelter,* the motive for the killings continued to elude the prosecution team for quite a while, and even when they discovered it, no one could quite believe it.

Manson had urged several of the cult members to go on a killing spree, telling them to make it look like the job of black militants. He'd formed this group from wayward kids in the Haight-Ashbury district of San Francisco, giving them a home on a rundown ranch outside Los Angeles and a sense of belonging. Many of them claimed to believe his notion that he was Christ (a name he took based on his last name, "Man's son," the Son of Man). His disciples were known as "the Family," and his vision of "Helter Skelter" (taken from a Beatles' song on their *White Album*) meant that blacks would rise up to massacre whites and reclaim the Earth.

"Helter Skelter," wrote Bugliosi from what he had learned from Susan Atkins, was supposedly to be the last war on the face of the Earth. However, the black race would need the help of a white tribal leader to govern things, and Manson was the man for the job. Toward that end, he prepared his small collective. Living on the ranch, he told them, would protect them from the final war, and in the end, when it was all over, the blacks would look to him to rule everything. Even though Bugliosi had pieced this all together, he was uncertain how it would play before a jury. Would anyone even believe it?

While Manson was suspected in numerous other murders, it was clear that he had manipulated his followers to do at least some of his killing for him—an act common to cult leaders who wish to act out violently. Bugliosi had to make the case in the 1970 trial that involved Manson and the three girls (who each had her own attorney) that since Manson was the group mastermind, he was as culpable as those who had raised their hands against the victims. And since he had no moral boundaries, he was dangerous in the extreme. In fact, it seemed to investigators that the slaughter had been a reaction to people in the entertainment industry who had rejected his music—a rather petty grievance for such a massive death toll. But one thing became clear throughout the seven-month trial for the four defendants: Manson was in charge and Manson had dictated what was to be done to the victims. Yet his cult members, both inside and outside the courtroom, stood up for him and fought hard to take the blame.

For Bugliosi, the trial was long, arduous, and uncertain, and was made more difficult by the antics of Manson's followers, by Manson's insistence that he was not getting a proper defense, by his intimidating behaviors, and even by President Nixon's public declaration that Manson was guilty. Yet the jury accepted the prosecutor's theory. In January 1971 they convicted Manson and two of the girls, Susan Atkins and Patricia Krenwinkel, of seven counts of first-degree murder. Leslie Van Houten was convicted on two counts of first-degree murder. In a separate trial that ended later that year, "Tex" Watson was convicted for his part.

Then came the sanity and penalty phase for Manson and the girls, in which the attorneys for the girls mounted a fierce defense based on their mental incapacities. Psychiatric evidence was entered regarding their states of mind at the time of the offense.

On March 4, Manson shaved his head, trimmed his beard into a fork, and announced, "I am the Devil and the Devil always has a bald head."

Various professionals came to the stand, including supposed experts on the effects on the brain of LSD ingestion. Dr. Keith Ditman said that taking the drug could make one more susceptible to someone's domination, although he conceded that not everyone has the same reaction. Another doctor admitted that violence is not generally a behavior of people on LSD.

All of the defendants were ultimately sentenced to death, but in 1972, California abolished the death penalty and commuted the sentences of all death-row inmates to life, which meant the possibility for parole. In 1974, Manson was diagnosed as "acute psychotic," and his antics in prison gave him a reputation as an incessant troublemaker.

The following year, Family member Lynette "Squeaky" Fromme attempted without success to assassinate President Gerald Ford. She got life in prison.

In explanation of the bizarre events in which the Manson cult was involved, Bugliosi set out to show that the three girls who committed the murders had possessed a syndrome of hostility and rage that preexisted their encounter with Manson but that was unleashed and manipulated by him. Each had some inner flaw that Manson had exploited, focusing on a common enemy their innate ability to be sadistically violent. He turned the victims into symbols of that enemy—the white establishment—and then commanded his followers to attack. His philosophy justified their actions and their own inner demons ensured that they would revel in it. There was no need, they were instructed, to feel regret.

In *Mass Murder*, Jack Levin and James Alan Fox offer the analysis of psychiatrist Clara Livesey, who stated that Manson operated in a way similar to other cult leaders, using his unique charisma to manipulate his followers. He developed a belief in them that he was invincible, even supernatural, and was aligned with Christ (might even *be* Christ). He gave them a cause that transformed them from nobodies into somebodies and assisted them to view their victims as symbolic and necessary sacrifices. The disciples felt special, and they vied for the honor of doing the most extreme acts as a way to acquire their leader's attention and approval. They were willing to take a fall for him, if need be. Manson had solved their problems and they owed him. He was their destiny—the only one they could envision. While they may not have had violence in mind when they joined the cult, they became part of a group mind, attuned and responsive to Manson.

In addition, by aligning themselves in this group mind, the responsibility for murder diffused throughout the entire group, shared by all, and thus became easier to bear for anyone who might suffer from pangs of conscience. Manson's vision and manipulation were not unlike one of the most nefarious political movements in the history of the world—one that had the means to carry out a destructive plan in a far more ambitious manner.

THE ULTIMATE EXPERIENCE

In the luxurious Wannsee House outside Berlin, a secret luncheon was laid out on January 20, 1942, in preparation for the arrival of fifteen of the top-ranking technocrats under the regime of Adolf Hitler. The chief of the Third Reich's security services, Reinhard Heydrich, had called the conference. Their agenda was "the final solution" to the "Jewish problem." While the plan to disenfranchise the Jews throughout Europe was already under way, with some mass shootings having been carried out, the general feeling in the group was that it was time for greater efficiency: There were so many people to be rid of—still eleven million—and it needed to be done more quickly.

The meeting was brief, lasting just over an hour. There was to be no record kept, but one person defied these orders and retained his notes, and it was from those documents that the world learned about the cold, rational discussion that resulted in the annihilation of millions of people. Heydrich had used a brilliant strategy. He neutralized the potential moral issues and the possible repugnancy among the luncheon guests with the meeting's general substance by writing the ideas in vague and dispassionate language. Nevertheless, the gist was clear: These men were there to approve the use of death camps ("work camps"), death in the gas chambers ("natural causes" or "emigration"), and disposal of remains in special crematoriums.

Speaking with one another in "amtssprache"—office talk—these bureaucrats acted as though they were merely part of a large machine at work, simply there to ensure that it continued to run. No one had been "responsible" for its initiation; they were only to see to its maintenance and increased speed. The final solution was to be managed with precision and economy, just like any job. No matter what was asked of anyone, it was reduced to a mundane activity with the idea that it was a matter of "company policy."

Years later, Adolph Eichmann, who had prepared Heydrich's speech that day, was asked about the Wannsee conference. He said that the reason for it was Heydrich's attempt to extend his scope of influence. To help him accomplish this goal, Eichmann was to make a general survey of the "operations" thus far on the question of Jewish "emigration." They had to stop allowing Jews to just leave, which only increased the ranks of the enemy, and to send many more Jews "east"—meaning to the concentration camps. There the able-bodied men were to be forced into a program known as "Vernichtung durch Arbeit," or "extermination via work." Those unable to work were simply killed, with the extermination activity categorized as a "special action." Heydrich proposed a specific means of "liquidation" and offered a prepared statistical report on how many people they could expect to "remove" in a specified amount of time. When later asked whether it was difficult for him to participate in sending so many people to their deaths, Eichmann responded, "To tell you the truth, it was easy. Our language made it easy."[2]

In part, Hitler's program was aided by superstitious beliefs that evolved into an obsession with the occult. The Ahnenerbe, an arm of the SS commissioned in the mid-1930s to research the ancestral heritage of the Aryan race, sought proof that only one race was meant to rule the world and that the Nazi vision of purification and world domination was supported by mythic forces. Heinrich Himmler saw his men as the reincarnation of Teutonic knights and kings, in particular King Arthur's knights. He designed Wewelsburg Castle to be their Camelot. On one floor they used a dark mosaic star that marked the center for occult rituals performed by twelve Nazi officers to channel the spirits of the deceased kings.

With the idea that blessings from Christ enveloped them, the Nazis felt justified to go on a massive killing spree against those who "contaminated" them. Theirs was a holy mission and nothing they could do in its service was wrong. What the world in retrospect deemed as one of the greatest evils perpetrated by human beings was viewed by those involved as a divine path that could not be denied. Killing those they deemed inferior was necessary to achieve the ultimate glory of the purification of the planet.

Besides bureaucrats and the military, Hitler also inspired some scientists and physicians to serve his horrific vision, most notably Auschwitz's "Angel of Death," Joseph Mengele. A leader in the Nazi biomedical vision, he thrived on experiments with genetic abnormalities. Arriving in Auschwitz on May 30, 1943, he took charge of the "selections" process. He'd show up at the prisoner transports looking quite elegant and at a glance would decide each person's destiny. He sent anyone with an imperfection to the gas chamber and singled others out for work or for his nefarious experiments.

Mengele was driven to uphold the Nazi ideal of racial purification. In his desire to improve the efficiency of the camp as a killing machine, he taught other doctors how to give phenol injections to a long line of prisoners, quickly ending their lives. He also shot people, and by some reports tossed live babies into the crematoria. Throughout all of this, he kept a detached, efficient demeanor and viewed himself as a "scientist."

In his book *The Nazi Doctors*, Robert Jay Lifton attempts to explain how physicians can actively participate in such a vision of death. The central mechanism is the ability to dissociate, which all people possess but which some exploit in such a way that they can perpetrate evil without recognizing that they are doing so. Lifton proposes the notion of "doubling," in which there exists a prior self—the original person before doubling takes place—and the doubled self—the one that emerges via dissociation and is nurtured within a specific culture. In other words, the person can dissociate from the moral demands of a situation to play another sort of role. He can prevent himself from seeing the nature of the act or its consequences. Lifton calls doubling the "Faustian bargain," because one sacrifices something of oneself to gain something one thinks one needs. Doubling, he says, is the division of the self into two functioning wholes, so that part of the self acts as the entire self.

This mechanism, while also operative in a dissociative identity disorder in which a person may have two or more functional personalities, is not to be confused as the same thing or as a schizoid-type of psychosis. The doctors were not like Sybil (at least as she was presented), having sixteen functional personalities. Instead, doubling is an adaptive mechanism in the human psyche that under certain conditions helps us to survive, and under other conditions allows us to have a private and a public self. It's like how psychopaths can participate in certain atrocious behaviors without feelings of remorse or concern about consequences. The doctor (or scientist or bureaucrat) who dissociates and doubles in order to kill learns to form a self-structure that allows his behavior. That is, he can redistribute his sense of morality to accommodate his killing by disavowing one part of himself with another. He can push the act from consciousness so that he may be aware of doing it but can sidestep the usual moral meaning of it.

Murder, then, is altered in its meaning by placing it in a morally justifiable context. The person involved gains something from it (pride in one's national loyalty, perhaps, or even survival within that culture), which reinforces the doubling behavior and ensures its continuation in the future. The doubled self can act autonomously but is still connected via personality structures to the prior self from which it arises. That is, a doctor can view himself as a compassionate, humane person, and a good family man, and still go out and kill. The killing self provides a means for the prior self to survive as much as possible without guilt. The killing self is the one doing the deeds, not the "real" self. In other words, in some cultures, people who must do certain things they might not ordinarily do, can take on the traits of a psychopath in order to perform.

Some people with doubled selves can only function that way in a limited environment, such as during a time of war. Others may take to this new existence with great enthusiasm and find they not only *can* kill but also like it. A few do experience guilt but cannot imagine a way out, so they continue.

Lifton believes that doctors as a group may be more susceptible to doubling than others, because they're used to skeletons and corpses, and because they learn to develop a "medical self" with a professional demeanor that may hide many things. They become inured to death and learn to function under many diverse demands. When done within the context of a heroic national vision, they also receive psychological support.

The idea of doubling has also been explored from another angle—the participation of ordinary people in destructive programs in a way that absolves them of moral responsibility. In another context, these same people might never have been violent.

PUPPETS

In the massacre of an entire hamlet in Vietnam in 1968, Lieutenant William Calley claimed that he was following orders. According to some accounts, he was responsible for giving the order to kill in a matter of three hours between four hundred and five hundred civilians who were unable to defend themselves, slaughtering women, babies, and the elderly without mercy. Some of his men raped and killed with abandon, and then afterward took a break for lunch. By their measure of success in that strange war, a body count of that magnitude was cause for celebration. While they all had been raised on quite different values, in the moment in that place they did what seemed right. In army circles, they had made an achievement and accomplished a goal. Back home in America, they were viewed with horror as savage killers.

Sociologist Fred Katz examined the ability of any given person to enact chilling evils in his book *Ordinary People and Extraordinary Evil.* He offered several explanatory factors. One of these was the human tendency to set extraordinary brutality apart from daily life as "unique" and not in the repertoire of behavior of most people. Katz believes that this cognitive act prevents us from seeing how evil can grow quite easily out of the ordinary. There are no special traits or behaviors, he points out, that might set malicious people apart as "monsters." In fact, most of the world's evil is actually done by ordinary people, and ironically those very same behaviors can assist us in living humanely. Defining evil as "behavior that deliberately deprives innocent people of their humanity, from small scale assaults on their dignity to outright murder," Katz focuses on how people actually behave.[3] Evil can beguile people. It can disguise itself so people view it in a much different light—one that permits them to manifest it. Hitler may have devised a wicked plan, but ordinary people zealously carried it out.

It works this way: Evil actions like outright massacre can be reinterpreted into acceptable behavior through certain frameworks, such as nationalism or "for science." Within that context, people who are addressing immediate problems may not see the larger context but may still contribute to its progress, whether by obeying a superior or taking incremental steps toward more atrocious behavior as part of career advancement. In addition, the evil behavior can be diffused throughout many people in a given culture so that no one person's cruelty stands out, and in those cultures that nurture cruelty, some evil acts may even be rewarded.

Katz talks about how the type of "packaging" can quietly organize life toward certain ideas and behaviors—even mass murder. Within certain visions, evil can become legitimate and those who are loyal to the cause can harm others as part of the cause. It's a "higher" good and those participants even view themselves as acting selflessly.

One thing that Katz does not discuss but that is often at play in the way organizations of people can harm others is the notion of "groupthink," a maladaptive form of group decisionmaking. Irving L. Janis, a Yale scholar, coined the term after studying the way decisions were made during the Bay of Pigs invasion and the escalation of the Vietnam War.

Groupthink begins when someone designs a stance and others join in and look to a leader, who then sets up a polarity: It's "us" against "them." We're morally right; they're morally wrong. Groupthink creates insular thinking inside the group and exaggerates external threats. The leader claims or implies that there is no better solution than his, he finds something external that helps him to exert pressure for group homogeneity, and no one is allowed to argue or question. Anyone who does gets vilified and mocked. It's a collective rationalization with self-appointed "mindguards" that stereotypes outsiders and makes it okay—sometimes even imperative—to sacrifice them. There's no real survey of alternatives or of the risks involved in the chosen option, and the boundaries soon close in around the group and become impermeable.

Katz does indicate that certain wartime atrocities had a similar dynamic. "The Vietnam package of values," he writes, "was a rearranged version of the peacetime American values on which most soldiers were brought up."[4] They knew not to kill innocent people, but they were able to reframe the Viet Cong as part of "them," and thus not innocent, even if civilian. The moral imperative not to kill was subordinated to other priorities within the same values package.

While there may exist people who are aroused by the infliction of torment and are happy for the open-ended license of war, there are those who do not love it but who will do it when the appropriate values context inspires them. According to Katz, they may be committed to only certain parts of a package, but will nevertheless carry on other activities demanded by the package as well. They can enact something like a massacre without being committed specifically to such egregious killing.

In a culture of cruelty or abuse, others can be exploited in any manner in which the leaders desire. The prevailing values allow it, even encourage it, and some within that culture flaunt their particular talent for it. Thus, acts of outright murder can become commonplace, even a way to gain status.

While motives to commit murder are clearly diverse, there are times when people become victims not because they are targets but simply because they are present. Mass murder can be committed as an extraneous activity along the way toward some other goal.

CHAPTER 10

Murder on the Side

I KNOW YOU LOVE ME

Someone who suffers from erotomania has a delusional belief that another person loves him (or her), no matter how vehement the other person's denials become—and even when there has been no contact at all. While most people who feel this overwhelming attachment do not become violent, some do.

At the rate of as many as two or three per week, Richard Farley wrote more than two hundred love letters to his young coworker Laura Black over a period of four years since they had met in 1984. Both worked at ESL, a California-based company. Sometimes he left the letters on her car and sometimes he delivered them to her mailbox. She apparently was not pleased, for she returned one unopened. He wasn't pleased with that, so he sent it back with a warning that she had better read it. What occurred from there is documented in Time-Life's *Mass Murderers*.

According to psychiatrist Doreen Orion in *I Know You Really Love Me*, a book about her own ordeal with a female patient suffering from erotomania, this delusion centers in control of the love object. Generally the delusion becomes an obsession and even a form of harassment through phone calls, unwanted gifts, letters, and constant surveillance. The obsessed person believes that he or she must know of the target person's whereabouts at all times. Sometimes this need for control builds into anger and can have fatal consequences for one or both parties, or even for a third party. People with this delusion are typically single, immature, unable to sustain close relationships, and attain otherwise unattainable relationships through fantasy. They mistake feelings in themselves for feelings in the other and have delusions that can last for many years. They seek any form of acknowledgment, even a restraining order, and may eventually become predatory. They idealize the other person and may view their own love as being so unique that they are above the law. Or they have no appreciation for the legal consequences of their actions.

Richard Farley, 35, hung around places where he knew he would catch a glimpse of Laura Black, including the area near where she lived and the campus where she took courses. He generally did not let her see him. As his obsession intensified, his letters indicated that he believed he owned her and that her life was within his power to take. At the very least, he could make her life miserable. All he wanted was a date, just a few moments of face-to-face time so that he could express his feelings to her. Within his delusion, it was likely that he believed she would find him so compelling that she would yield.

Black had tried unsuccessfully to dissuade Farley in his pursuit, and at the time, little was known about the mind of a stalker. The first antistalking laws would not come into effect until 1991 after John Bardo shot and killed actress Rebecca Schaffer. (He, too, professed an abiding love for his love object.) Most people believed that to get some distance, it was sufficient to tell such a relentless admirer that they did not share that person's feelings and would like to be left alone.

But that's not the way a stalker operates. His (or her) target person has no will of her own; she is a pawn in *his* game. While most stalkers are not violent, those situations in which the stalker and stalkee have had prior friendly contact or a relationship tend to have higher risk. The reason appears to be that the stalkee's acknowledgment of the stalker has offered some hope, which intensifies the feelings and the belief that some type of relationship is possible between them. While there's no documentation to this effect, it's likely that when Black and Farley met she was at least cordial, and this kind of gesture can be sufficient reason for a stalker to infuse his fantasy with certain emotional expectations.

Dr. J. Reid Meloy, author of *Violent Attachments* and editor of *The Psychology of Stalking,* is an expert on stalking behavior. Pathological attachments, he says, most often occur in males and they follow a fairly predictable progression. There is initial contact, after which feelings of infatuation develop. The love object is deified and is thus considered perfect and unattainable. The stalker then begins to approach the object, but also sets himself up for rejection (because he's not worthy), which then triggers the delusion through which he projects his own feelings onto the object. He also develops intense anger to mask his shame, which fuels the obsessive pursuit and the desire to control the object through harassment or injury. Violence is most likely to occur when the love object is devalued, as through behavior that defies the ideal or through an imagined betrayal.

Black was an electrical engineer at ESL, while Farley worked in software. At first she tried to be nice about her rejection, but when Farley continued to pursue her and leave her small gifts, she became rude. She even moved several times, but Farley always found her again. When Farley pushed her against a wall, she filed a sexual harassment suit against him, and the company fired him. Farley, a navy veteran and gun collector, did not take that lightly. Nor did it stop his surveillance activities. In fact, without a job, he had more time to pursue them.

Early in 1988, Black got a temporary restraining order, which finally sent Farley into action. On February 16, he armed himself with a gas mask, numerous loaded guns, a knife, and several cans of flammable liquid. Then he showed up outside ESL. Taking an assault rifle, two shotguns, and several pistols with him, he entered the building. On his way in he killed two men, and by the time he reached Black's office, he had killed five more workers. Confronting Black, he shot her, but despite her critical wounds she would survive.

Farley walked away, his need to inflict damage diminishing, and the police were already responding. They surrounded the building while he barricaded himself in with hundreds of rounds of ammunition ready for use. To police officers who communicated with him by phone, he indicated that he'd just wanted to take Black out on one date. He had meant only to damage computers, not kill anyone. It had just happened. He requested a sandwich, a soda, and a priest, and then turned himself in.

At his trial, Farley was convicted of seven counts of first-degree murder and given the death penalty. He claimed that he'd gone to ESL that day to kill himself as a way to make Black feel guilty over her rejections. Instead, he killed other people—victims he had not even targeted. He'd just acted out in violence while attempting to achieve a different goal.

While Farley is clearly not to be grouped among those workers who return to punish a company, his choice of the place where he planned to punish Black or get her attention was likely symbolic. This was the company where he had been employed and from which he had been fired—in his mind due to her. So while he claimed that the massacre was a miscalculation, his actions said otherwise. Black was part of the company that he perceived had caused his life to go into a downward spiral, and there was probably at least an unconscious desire to inflict real damage against all of those who had frustrated him.

And it's not just relentless stalkers who commit such acts of violence. Sometimes it's merely a jealous boyfriend, and in the next incident, the mass killer had no personal association to the place where he took so many lives.

THE DEVIL GOT INTO ME

Julio Gonzales, 36, was considered by those who knew him to be a pathologically jealous man. Once he was in a relationship, he considered that he owned and controlled the woman. Such was the case with Lydia Feliciano. She entered into a relationship with him in New York City and although it was fraught with trouble, she managed to stay in it for seven years. In 1990, fed up with Gonzales's demanding ways, Feliciano broke up with him. She asked him to leave her alone so she could get on with her life.

But Gonzales did not accept that a woman who once had yielded to him could make this decision. He made repeated attempts to get her back, but each time he failed. That only added fuel to the flame of his anger. He knew where she worked, so he devised a plan to punish her for her rejection. If he could not have her, she would have to die.

Feliciano worked at the Happy Land social club, located in the Bronx. It was a place where people could dance all night, even though the building was substandard for such gatherings. In the event of fire, there were few escape routes, the stairways from the upper floor were steep and narrow, and there was only one functional door, which was located on the ground floor. Nevertheless, each night people came and packed themselves into the club to meet others and to have a good time. It was illegal to allow such unsafe conditions, but the club owners turned a blind eye.

On March 25, 1990, Gonzales was fuming. He decided to make one more attempt at reconciliation. He waited through that night and into the early morning hours before making his move. At the club, he offered Feliciano one more chance to make up with him and come back, but she still refused. They argued and Gonzales was tossed out. He vowed that he would return, and so he did. But even as he left, Lydia slipped out the door to go home.

Around 3:30 in the morning, Gonzales purchased gas from a gas station near the club, carried it in a plastic container back to the building, and poured it around the bottom of the door. Then he lit a match and watched the wooden structure catch fire. As it spread, Gonzales crossed the street to observe the panic, satisfied that his former girlfriend would perish.

Instead, he killed a great many others who had nothing to do with his obsession. Although the fire department responded to the growing blaze in haste, people were trapped inside. Only five managed to get out of the single exit, engulfed in flames, while sixty-one men and twenty-six women died in the building, from being trampled in the panic, from smoke inhalation, and from burns.

Before the day was over, Gonzales was found where he lived. He smelled strongly of gasoline fumes, so he was arrested. Under interrogation, his explanation was, "I got angry. The devil must have gotten into me and I set the place on fire."[1] He was charged with eighty-seven counts of murder, along with arson and numerous counts of depraved indifference to human life.

As the trial approached, Gonzales wanted the authorities to believe he had been insane at the time, but it was too late. He had already made a confession in which he'd admitted that he had known ahead of time that he was going to do some damage. Later he tried to say that a voice had commanded him to do it, but two mental health professionals for the prosecution insisted that he was malingering. Yet two psychologists for the defense indicated that he had indeed experienced temporary psychosis.

The jury decided that he was sane at the time of the crime, and they convicted him. For each count, he received twenty-five years to life, to be served concurrently (as dictated by New York law). Relatives of the victims were devastated that the sentence had not been harsher.

In *Flash Point*, Michael Kelleher characterizes this incident as one of perverted love, the result of a man who insists that he must control the person he believes he loves. Kelleher analyzed the crime as one of revenge and retribution. Gonzales was unable to accept that Feliciano had a mind of her own, and in his rage and frustration over his inability to make her obey him, eighty-seven people had needlessly died a terrible death. It was a massacre of unprecedented proportions, and yet was not even the killer's ultimate aim.

Even while offenders like Gonzales attempt to shift the blame to a mental illness, some people who kill for reasons other than to cause specific people to die certainly are psychotic. The next incident is a case in point. While psychosis was covered in Chapter 4, in this case the mass murderer had a unique goal in which the deaths were incidental.

MURDER FOR BLOOD

Richard Trenton Chase drank blood from living creatures because he was afraid of disintegrating. He was institutionalized several times, as documented in *Whoever Fights Monsters* by former FBI agent Robert Ressler, who interviewed him. Chase was even dubbed "Dracula" by hospital staff over his habit of killing birds like the lunatic character Renfield from Bram Stoker's novel.

Chase was preoccupied with any sign that something was wrong with him, and he once entered an emergency room looking for someone whom he believed had stolen his pulmonary artery. He also complained that the bones were coming out through the back of his head, his stomach was situated backward, and his heart often stopped beating. Nevertheless, doctors tended to view him as more of a hypochondriac than a potential offender.

Eventually Chase was released from confinement and deemed no longer a danger. He moved into an apartment, without real supervision, and began to catch and torture cats, dogs, and rabbits. He apparently killed them to drink their blood. But animal blood was not good enough. He soon began seeking larger prey. Toward this end, he acquired a gun.

Early in 1978, after he'd shot a man in a drive-by incident just to see what it was like, he entered the home of Teresa Wallin, 22 and three months pregnant. To his mind, since her door had been unlocked, it was an open invitation to come in and take whatever he needed. He shot Wallin twice and, after she fell to the floor and died, dragged her body down a hall and into the bedroom. With a knife, he stabbed her repeatedly. Among other atrocities, he also cut out her kidneys and severed her pancreas in two. Then he got a yogurt container from the trash and apparently used it to drink her blood. He left the cup and the knife there.

Not long afterward, Chase went on a rampage, killing a number of victims at once. On January 27, Chase entered another unlocked home in the middle of the day and killed Evelyn Miroth, 38; a male friend who was visiting her; and her 6-year-old son, Jason. He also grabbed her infant son from his cradle, smashed the boy's head in the bathroom, and took the body with him when he left. Back at his apartment, he removed the head and consumed several of the organs before dumping the body in a box into an alley.

The police received assistance from FBI profilers, and they quickly closed in and arrested Chase one day as he was leaving his apartment. They found evidence that he had used blenders to chop up organs and that he may have been planning a series of murders across the rest of the year. In fact, his living conditions were quite dire, with evidence that he had consumed both human and animal tissues raw. Around the place police found numerous pet collars from cats and dogs.

In prison, Chase told another inmate that he needed the blood of his victims because of blood poisoning, and he'd grown tired of hunting for animals. He indicated to Ressler in a private interview that he was afraid that his blood was turning to powder from "soap dish poisoning." Clearly he was psychotic, and his fatal offenses had been perpetrated in the interest of a delusional idea about self-preservation, but a California jury nevertheless found him sane. Chase was convicted of six counts of first-degree murder and sentenced to be executed. Instead he died a few years later in his cell from a drug overdose.

LEAVE NO ONE ALIVE

Sometimes murder is not the ultimate goal, but it just goes along with the offender's vision of the real crime, such as eliminating witnesses during a robbery. If many witnesses are present, it can become a mass murder.

The Wah Mee gambling club in Seattle, Washington, was a historic speakeasy where affluent restaurateurs and businessmen in the Chinese community would congregate. Winners could take home quite a lot of money and losers could lose just as big. Willie Mak, a recent immigrant, had racked up quite a debt in another gambling club where he worked. He decided to end his troubles with a heist at the Wah Mee Club. He invited his high school friend, Benjamin Ng, in on the deal, as well as another immigrant, Tony Ng (no relation to Benjamin).

While Tony kept a lookout, the other two men entered the Wah Mee Club just before midnight on February 18, 1983, and ordered the fourteen customers and employees present to the floor. After tying them up and robbing them, Mak and Ng decided to leave no witnesses. They shot all fourteen men in the head, and walked away with several thousand dollars.

But one victim, 62-year-old Wai Chin, survived. He managed to free himself and go find help. He was also able to identify the three perpetrators, and two of them, Willie Mak and Benjamin Ng, were quickly apprehended. Tony Ng fled the country to Canada.

Mak and Ng were tried for the massacre and, based on the eyewitness report, convicted. Mak received the death penalty, but his sentence was later commuted to life. Ng received a life sentence as well. Two years later, Tony Ng was extradited from Canada, where he had been hiding, and he was tried as well. Although the jury apparently believed his tale of being coerced to participate, he was found guilty of robbery and assault.

Much more recently, a similar slaughter occurred across the country, but apparently for gang-related motives. In one of the worst mass killings in the history of Philadelphia, Pennsylvania, on December 28, 2000, ten people were shot in a Lex Street building by masked intruders with semiautomatic guns. Seven of them died while three survived but were badly wounded. Given the crack house neighborhood and the likelihood that the address was a drug den, the obvious motive to the police was drug trade rivalry, and soon four young dealers were charged. One man who knew the victims confessed and implicated the others, but then said his confession had been coerced. No physical evidence linked any of them to the crime, but since they seemed the likely perpetrators, and since pressure was strong to close the case, they were sent to jail. Then a survivor who had failed to identify them at the time found a psychiatrist to enhance her memory, which helped her to finger two of the suspects.

It seemed an open-and-shut case. But then a gun was taken from a man named Shihean Black, unrelated to the other four men, which ballistics identified as one of the murder weapons. Upon hearing this from investigators, Black's first reaction was to vomit. Then he confessed. Later he recanted. Then he confessed and recanted again. Despite having the gun and detailed knowledge of the crime scene, he wasn't charged. In other words, he was an annoying loose end on a case already "solved"— a case that had received national attention.

Eventually, another man, Dawud Faruqi, claimed to know something and he recalled Black having the gun just before the shooting. Yet Faruqi had a proven record as a liar, so the police still did not act. They kept the other four suspects in prison for eighteen months, under threat of seeking the death penalty at trial.

Yet the day before the trial was to start, the district attorney, due to lack of evidence, was forced to let the men go. Investigators then concentrated on another gang—one in which Dawud Faruqi and his brother, Khalid, were members. So were Black and another man, Bruce Veney. Under interrogation, Veney and Black confessed and pleaded guilty. In March 2004 the Faruqi brothers were convicted on seven counts of first-degree murder. Apparently, the massacre was the result of a robbery attempt gone bad.

Whether the reason is perverted love, robbery, gang violence, or something else, sometimes the mind of the mass murderer is concentrated not on death and destruction but on something quite different. Yet these incidents cannot be ignored in a study of the phenomenon of mass murder. Some executions are planned, while some occur in the moment; but in any event, they are typically perpetrated by people with access to weapons who clearly don't hesitate to use them, no matter what the body count. In such cases, the idea of the disgruntled white male loner who acts out of frustration to wreak havoc is entirely irrelevant. The mass murderer may be someone merely inclined to prove his perverse idea of love, to act out a delusion, or to enrich himself.

Given the wide range of motives and types of mass murder that we've looked at throughout this study, what can we really say about the causes and risk factors? Is there a way to anticipate and possibly to prevent at least some massacres in the future? The answer lies in knowledge and early intervention.

CHAPTER 11

Stress, Murder, Madness, and Risk Assessment

THEORIES

It's one thing to know the details of cases involving mass murder, and it's quite another to be able to distill from them the prognostic red flags associated with those who might one day develop into mass murderers. One thing is clear: We do not yet know what behaviors in particular will predict murder or mass murder. We can only say that there are some behaviors that seem to show up in these incidents more than others, and those behaviors can be linked to a collection of factors that appear to be statistically significant in risk assessment studies. Here I'll cover some of these signals and offer ideas that professional threat assessment groups have developed from their work with potential violence in schools, workplaces, and communities as they attempt to pinpoint troubled people and to decrease their stress and their impulse to act out. No one claims to be able to predict with a high degree of accuracy, but some programs offer guidelines for helping those who need to be watchful.

Many criminologists and forensic psychologists have theories about what combination of factors are likely to precipitate violence of the magnitude evident in mass murders. Essentially, they look to those conditions that seem clearly to form and maintain a mind that can ponder fatal assaults against others, and the development of that psychology generally begins with frustrations experienced during childhood.

According to John Monahan and H. J. Steadman in *Violence and Mental Disorder*, such research must meet seven criteria: (1) "dangerousness" must be segregated into component parts: risk factors, harm, and likelihood of occurrence; (2) a rich array of risk factors must be assessed from multiple domains; (3) harm must be scaled in terms of seriousness and assessed with multiple measures; (4) the probability estimate of risk must be acknowledged to change over time and context; (5) priority must be given to actuarial research; (6) the research must be done in large and broadly representative samples; and (7) the goal must be management as well as assessment.

Monahan claims that all of the criteria are met in the MacArthur Violence Risk Assessment Study, in which a team of experts examined the relationship between mental disorder and violent behavior directed against others. Over more than a decade, they utilized ongoing interviews with patients, interviews with collateral individuals, and official sources of information such as hospital records. Noting that most studies suffer from limitations, such as too few factors or weak criterion measures, they devised a comprehensive list of risk factors (134) across four domains (dispositional/personal, historical, contextual, and clinical) that (1) have been associated with violence in prior research, (2) are believed by experienced clinicians to be associated with violence, and (3) are hypothesized to be associated with violence by existing theories of violence or mental disorder. This included factors not previously studied, such as social support, impulsiveness, anger control, psychopathy, and delusions. Experts in these fields developed risk assessment instruments, such as the Psychopathy Checklist-Revised (PCL-R), to assist with measurement and prediction. The goal was to do the best science possible and to offer a viable tool for clinical risk assessment.

Of the four domains, only contextual and clinical factors were deemed relevant to risk management, because these factors could be changed. But among those factors that were most potent for violence were the following: being male, having a prior record of violence or aggression, experiencing physical abuse in childhood, having a parent who was a substance abuser or criminal, living in a disadvantaged neighborhood, having a diagnosis of an adjustment disorder or substance abuse, exhibiting evidence of psychopathy (the strongest factor), having a suspicious attitude toward others, experiencing an auditory hallucination that commanded a violent act, thinking or fantasizing about harming others, and having a high score on the Novaco Anger Scale.

The latest update on the MacArthur Violence Risk Assessment Study indicates that, compared to other instruments that assess those who are already hospitalized, its results appear to be highly accurate. However, it is computationally complex and time-consuming. It relies on tree-based prediction models that involve a lot of questions to answer, but computer software that makes it manageable for clinicians and threat assessment groups is available.

Applied to mass killers, a look at their backgrounds makes it clear that many of them behaved in ways that, in retrospect, indicated that one day they might explode. Inability to deal with stress—for example, veiled threats and angry outbursts or retaliations against others—was a factor. The buildup of frustration appears to derive from the way they learned (or did not learn) to manage anger and stress. In essence, that's rooted in how their observations of role models blend with their response to the teaching strategies of those responsible for their development and their own individual cognitive processing. In others words, thanks to the uniqueness of the individual, children subjected to similar conditions and treatment can come away from them with quite different behaviors. Yet those who experience higher exposure to violence in the environment appear to have a greater tendency to duplicate it, especially if they have military experience later in life.

This is not to say that angry children will turn into killers or that passive children will not. There is no clear causal relationship between the child and the adult when it comes to predicting violence, but since behavioral patterns in adapting to stress can point toward the potential for more serious problems down the line, it can still be helpful to identify those individuals in need of anger management and other forms of counseling.

Michael Kelleher, in *Flash Point*, views the evolution of an obsessive fantasy as central to the development of a person into a mass murderer. "The consideration and thought that are given to the crime," he writes, "are often in the form of unrelenting and hostile fantasies of a long-standing nature."[1] The fantasy becomes an obsession mixed with the need for domination and control, and when it evolves into the act of actually planning an incident, the final act of annihilation is more likely to occur than if there's no clear planning. Some fantasies are victim-specific, while others may seek a symbolic target—and yet even the victim-specific attacks may actually bring harm to someone else. Some killers are focused, while others may kill indiscriminately. Some know exactly what they are doing, others do not—even as they stand amid the bodies. Some incidents have clear causal factors, while others appear to be altogether inexplicable.

The fantasy itself may begin early in life, because the person has been unable during childhood to deal with life's inevitable punches. Rather than bend and adjust, such people grow angry, frustrated, disappointed, and possibly withdrawn. They may feel victimized, and so they develop an inflated sense of self-worth to compensate, which contributes to a belief in their entitlement. They also blame others for their problems. These others then become obstacles, which results in an increased sense of life's unfairness.

The potential offender must destroy others before they hinder or destroy him. Those others are devalued as meaningless, and this person becomes driven by his need to maintain control. He "typically depersonalizes at the moment of attack." Some mass killers have already killed, such as those experienced with warfare, and thus depersonalization may come more easily. In any event, his life is worth more than those of his victims, and they must be exploited to give him back his sense of control.

Findings from studies of criminals have been instructive as well. Dr. Lonnie Athens, author of *The Creation of Dangerous Violent Criminals*, believes that antisocial behavior develops through specific steps. He theorizes that people start off benign, so in an attempt to discover why only some people in a crime-vulnerable environment turn violent, he interviewed violent criminals in prisons to find out what they had in common. From his research, he determined that people become violent through four stages of what he terms "violentization":

- brutalization and subjugation,
- belligerency,
- violent coaching, and
- criminal activity.

First, the person (usually a child) becomes a victim of violence and feels powerless to avoid it. So he experiences fear and humiliation. He may also be bullied or subjected to repeated violence. Then he is taught how and when to become violent (often by a person who was violent to him) and how to profit from it. It's not long before he's had sufficient exposure to such role models to act on the impulse to take charge and inflict what was inflicted on him.

According to Athens, if someone who comes from a violent environment does not become violent, it's because some part of the process is missing. Athens seems to neglect the individualized aspects involved, such as an inherent tendency toward aggression, narcissism, or shallow emotions—any of which may turn out to be physiologically determined. Yet this theory does help us to understand why some people are resilient in the face of life's difficulties and others decide that the only way to act is to react—violently.

Dr. Stanton E. Samenow, an authority on the criminal personality and a former member of Reagan's task force on crime victims, insists that a criminal's way of thinking is vastly different from that of responsible people, and that the "errors of logic" derive from a pattern of behavior that begins in childhood. Criminals, he says, *choose* crime by rejecting society and preferring the role of a victimizer. This appears to be consistent with the perspective of many mass murderers. While they control of their own actions, they assign the blame for their behavior to others. Thus they have no insight about their intentions. They devalue people and exploit others insofar as those others can be manipulated toward ends to which the criminals feel entitled. They don't learn to respond more appropriately because they'd don't think correctly.

Some theorists look specifically at the earliest years of a child's development to understand how he may become violent in later years. According to Robin Karr-Morse and Meredith S. Wiley in *Ghosts from the Nursery,* the roots of violence develop in the first two years of life, starting at conception. With the exception of certain head injuries, they claim, there is no specific biological or sociological factor that predisposes a child to violence. It appears from the research that a predisposition to violence develops from the interaction of multiple factors.

In other words, according to their theory, violence does not derive from a negative experience, a brain disorder, genetics, or mistakes in parenting, but it could be the result of the cumulative effect of a combination of factors, along with the failure of normal protective systems in the environment. Among those factors associated with violence, they list harmful substances ingested by mothers during pregnancy, chronic maternal stress during pregnancy, low birth weight, early maternal rejection or abuse, nutritional deficiencies, a low verbal IQ, and trouble with attention deficit and hyperactivity.

While none of these factors is considered clearly to be causal, in certain combinations and with certain dispositions they can provoke anger, thwart the development of anger management skills, and trigger impulsive violence against self or others. If kids fail to connect early with caregivers, there can be problems later in life. Babies reflect back into the world whatever they absorb, the authors state, and that notion has serious implications. If we fail to address the issues of competent child-rearing and healthy pregnancies, one in twenty babies born today will end up behind bars.

Debra Niehoff, a neuroscientist, studied twenty years' worth of research before she wrote *The Biology of Violence.* She offers perhaps the most inclusive theory, but also one that would involve the most expensive intervention, as the causes of violence appear to be entirely individualized. Specifically, as Niehoff read through all the literature, she wanted to know whether violence was the result of genes or the environment. In her opinion, both biological and environmental factors are involved, and each modifies the other, such that processing a situation toward the end of a violent resolution is unique to each individual. In other words, a particular type of stimulation or overload in the brain is not necessarily going to cause violence in every instance. It's a matter of how that individual has developed his or her view of the environment.

The way the process works, she says, is that the brain keeps track of our experiences through chemical codes. When we have an interaction (relational or environmental) we develop a neurochemical profile that affects our attitudes. Each new experience either affirms the profile or shifts it in some manner. In other words, if a child is brutalized, the world will seem unsafe and she may approach others with a sense of guardedness and suspicion. Then if the next person betrays or attacks her, she is affirmed in her suspicions and the profile is reinforced. But if the next person instead provides a positive experience, the profile may shift to influence a slightly different attitude—that sometimes the world is safe and trustworthy.

However we feel about these things will set off certain emotional reactions and the chemistry of those feelings is translated into our responses. Once we put a certain behavior out there, the other person reacts and we have an emotional response to their reaction, which in turn affects our brain chemistry. Every interaction updates our neurochemical profile.

The chemistry of aggression is associated with the chemistry of our attitudes, and we may turn a normally appropriate response into an inappropriate response by overreaction or by directing it at the wrong person. In other words, the person's ability to properly evaluate the situation may become impaired, setting them up to be treated in just the way they expect—even if the other person had no intention of doing so. Niehoff says that there are different patterns of violent behavior and that certain physiological differences are associated with each pattern. Some people are overreactive, some are balanced, and some are underreactive. The overreactor develops poor focus while the underreactor has trouble developing empathy. Either pattern will affect how others interact with that person, and thus will affect the neurochemical profile.

The development of violence thus results from a cumulative exchange between a person's experiences and the nervous system. It all gets coded into the body's neurochemistry as a sort of emotional record. The record remains intact, affecting behavior, until such time as experience influences a change. Given that many mass murderers were known to have rather rigid temperaments, it becomes clear why their fantasies about being picked on or thwarted can remain intact long enough to result in explosive violence.

Children who grow up around violence are at risk for pathological development that can issue in future violence. Infants and toddlers need to develop trust and a feeling of safety in order to have healthy development. If they don't have good relationships in the home, they will have a more difficult time in any type of association outside the home.

Then during the school years, children develop the social skills they need to function as adults. Violence in their environment hinders this, and may even adversely affect it. A lack of feeling of safety harms cognitive functioning, which affects schoolwork, and children who live in fear often repress their feelings, which thwarts their ability to empathize. Violence in the home or neighborhood may handicap them right from the start. They also have a difficult time concentrating, and feelings of helplessness may pervade their lives. In addition, constant stress in the environment can produce the symptoms of posttraumatic stress disorder, which will affect how much rest they get and how well they cope.

To reiterate, from studies that examine the correlates, there is a relationship between certain factors and the risk of future violence among adolescents. Those factors include past violent behavior, substance abuse, aggressive peers, family aggression, social stress, character disorders, focused anger, and a low degree of resilience. During the first three to nine months, an infant develops bonds with the parent. Some infants are easy, some difficult. Parents must deepen this bond, because a strong factor in the development of antisocial behavior is the child's lack of connection with others, which then may manifest as an adjustment disorder. Self-worth, resilience, hope, intelligence, and empathy are essential to building character for effective impulse control, anger management, and conflict resolution. Without these skills, children cannot establish rewarding relationships with community systems.

Kids who act aggressively to solve their problems actually solve nothing. Society needs to grasp the fact that children can form an intent to kill whether or not they understand what they're doing. That means they can begin to develop early those fantasies that may one day issue in mass murder. Any sign of a lack of empathy or of devaluing another person's life must be noticed early and treated, not ignored. Through television programming and videogames, we're teaching kids to kill with a great degree of accuracy and to think of killing as an appropriate means to an end. Since it's unlikely that the programming will change significantly in years to come (because violence sells), we need to attend better to the danger signs. If we don't, those children will grow into adults who view assault as a quick and easy way to solve their problems.

SPECIFIC SIGNALS

Different levels of risk are associated with different types of threats. When threats to return for "payback" are vague, implausible, inconsistent, or indirect, with no specific targets mentioned, this is considered low risk. The risk level rises with specific details and with evidence of actual planning. A medium-level risk threat would be a plan that could be carried out, but for which indicators of the place and time remain vague or general. Yet when preparatory steps are clear and the threatener has access to weapons, the threat now becomes high risk. Those messages that are direct, specific, credible, and show planning are the ones to take most seriously. For example, Charles Whitman, who had access to weapons, indicated he had recurring fantasies of climbing up the University of Texas's clock tower and shooting people from it. If there has been any amount of surveillance of the target, chances are better that the person may indeed act. While not all mass killers telegraph their intent via threats, many do, and when they do, their words should be evaluated for the likelihood that they are ready to do what they are threatening.

Among the specific traits or behaviors that provide a constellation of red flags for the potential for violence in adults or kids (and should not be construed as sufficient in themselves but as participant factors in an interactive collection) are:

- a preoccupation with themes of violence, especially attention to other such incidents on the news or in the papers,
- low frustration tolerance and few or no behaviors that indicate resilience,
- significant stressors, such as broken relationships, loss, humiliation, or a number of such incidents in quick succession,
- tendency to "collect" injustices,
- tendency to blame others for life's unfairness,
- the ability to dehumanize others,
- withdrawal and alienation,
- poor coping skills,
- sense of superiority or entitlement,
- low self-esteem,
- excessive need for attention,
- intolerance and rigidity, especially in an atmosphere of change,
- suspiciousness and paranoia,
- substance abuse,
- mental instability that involves aggression, and
- avid collection of weapons or expressed fantasies about war or assault.

While no single factor or trait has been found to be causal, there is reason to believe that many mass murderers share a number of these traits, so finding many together in one person who appears to be having diffi-culty dealing with anger should signal that this is a person in need of some type of intervention *before* he or she grows violent.

RISK MANAGEMENT

Most threat assessment and risk management has been done in the context of assisting companies with potentially violent employees or schools with troubled students, but some assessments have been done on a smaller scale, such as with stalker evaluations. In addition, the government has funded the development of programs for evaluating the future potential for terrorist activities, in addition to putting programs in place after the Branch Davidian fiasco to better handle potentially violent cults.

In *The Unknown Darkness*, for example, Gregg McCrary discusses the longest standoff in law enforcement history, which occurred between the FBI and the Freemen, a well-armed, right-wing Christian identity group in Montana. Having learned lessons from Waco, in this case the FBI did not try to establish an armed perimeter around the Freemen, and they dispensed with military assault-type tactics and equipment.

"Instead," writes McCrary, "they developed and followed a unified plan that coordinated tactical and negotiation strategy. During what turned out to be the standoff's last few days, the power to the Freemen's com-pound was cut, but that was done in support of negotiations, rather than in spite of them. After 81 days, the Freemen, who had threatened to kill FBI Agents and other law enforcement officers, surrendered quietly, leav-ing over 100 guns inside their compound. Not a shot was fired, and no one was injured."[2]

He points out that by coordinating mutually supportive techniques and strategies, and attempting to respect the people involved rather than treating them as enemies that needed to be taken out, violence was averted.

On a lesser scale, while no company, school, or person can ever be entirely free from risk from someone who intends harm, and while there will always be violence motivated by some irrational impulse, there are ways to diminish the danger.

A company, for example, can avoid firing people during high-stress periods, such as Christmas holidays. It can also try to determine what most raises the target employee's anxiety level and seek to find a way to address it peacefully, such as assisting him or her with the job search process. If a potentially violent employee is terminated, then security, coworkers, and local police should be notified.

Some companies have instituted programs of preincident training—that is, rehearsing what each person should do in the event of the return of a violent employee. In addition, they have opened anonymous lines of communication for people to report rumors of violence or outright threats. Getting these things documented can help the personnel department to see the patterns and take steps to diminish the buildup of frustration in a specific employee. Companies may also offer training in self-defense.

In the event that a person is having trouble but is not going to be fired, certain programs may include that person in activities so that he or she does not feel so isolated. Any rumors about employee harassment should be investigated, since it's clear that a number of mass murders have occurred as the result of a person feeling bullied, picked on, or ridiculed.

Discipline needs to be even and fair. Although some people will always view themselves as victimized, it still helps if a supervisor or teacher can point to instances of similar treatment toward others.

At schools, while "outsider" behaviors are no indication of future trouble, and thus should not be used as the basis to single kids out, neither should teachers or counselors ignore clearly troubling behaviors, such as bullying, withdrawal, or signs of depression.

Whether in the company or school environment, counselors or managers can assist in developing anger management programs. While not everyone will respond to these efforts (the school shooters at Columbine High School did not), it's still possible to assist those who do see that they may have a problem and who desire to overcome it. They can then address the changes in their own stress levels and seek appropriate help.

Counselors can also be attuned to specific stressors, such as divorce, death in the family, demoralization, or other incidents that threaten a person's sense of self-esteem. People in the workplace or at school should know what resources are available to talk through their difficulties, and should be made to feel comfortable using them.

In the event of an incident, those groups who are affected by it (co-workers, friends, and relatives) should have access to appropriate counseling and other types of assistance. In addition, when people are fired or laid off, their concerns need to be addressed, and they may potentially need help in adjusting and in managing stress.

While incidents of mass murder show a range of contexts and precipitators, making it more difficult to develop a clear understanding of their causes, it's nevertheless generally clear that pent-up frustration and anger play a significant role, as well as the attitude that others are to blame. The better our attempts to develop stress tolerance strategies for people at risk, the more likely it is that we can avert at least some potential incidents of mass murder.

Notes

INTRODUCTION

1. Michael D. Kelleher, *Flash Point* (Westport, Conn.: Praeger, 1997), p. 2.

CHAPTER 1

1. Roxy di Marco, "Slayer Missed His First Target," *Philadelphia Inquirer,* September 7, 1949, p. 1.

2. "'I Ran Out of Bullets So I Went Home,' Killer Says," *Philadelphia Inquirer,* September 6, 1949, p. 1.

3. "Besieged Slayer Talks with Reporter on Phone," *Philadelphia Inquirer,* September 6, 1949, p. 1.

4. "Mad Camden Veteran Shoots 12 Dead and Wounds 4 in Murder Orgy," *Philadelphia Inquirer,* September 7, 1949, pp. 1, 2.

5. Ibid.

6. Meyer Berger, "Veteran Kills 12 in Mad Rampage on Camden Street," *New York Times,* September 6, 1949, p. 1.

7. "Madman Traces His Murder Path," *Philadelphia Inquirer,* September 7, 1949, p. 1.

8. "Killer 'Changed' by War Service," *New York Times,* September 7, 1949, p. 1.

9. "Madman Traces His Murder Path," p. 1.

10. "Mad Camden Killer Spirited Away to State Asylum in Trenton," *Philadelphia Inquirer,* September 8, 1949, continued from p. 1.

11. "Unruh Found Mad, Escapes Trial as Killer," *Philadelphia Inquirer,* October 8, 1949, p. 1.

12. Personal interview with Richard Noll, May 2002.

CHAPTER 2

1. Bob Greene, "The Voice of Richard Speck," *Chicago Tribune*, December 8, 1978.
2. Robert K. Ressler and Tom Shachtman, *Whoever Fights Monsters* (New York: St. Martin's Press, 1992),p. 71.
3. The film is shown as part of the documentary, "Richard Speck," produced by the A&E Network in 2001.

CHAPTER 3

1. Jack Levin and James Alan Fox, *Mass Murder: America's Growing Menace* (New York: Plenum, 1985), p. 32.
2. Robert Hare, *Without Conscience: The Disturbing World of the Psychopaths Among Us* (New York: Pocket, 1993), p. ix.
3. David Freed, "'Going Hunting Humans,' Slayer Told Wife," *Los Angeles Times*, July 20, 1984, p. 1.
4. Ibid.
5. Ibid.

CHAPTER 4

1. "Mass Murder: An American Tragedy," A&E Network documentary, 1996.
2. *Mass Murderers* (New York: Time-Life Books, 1992), p. 79.
3. "Long Island Railroad Massacre," A&E Network documentary, 1996.
4. Ibid.
5. Eshleman, Russell, Mark Butler, and David Lee Presston, "Woman Opens Fire on Shoppers at Springfield Mall," *Philadelphia Inquirer*, October 31, 1985, p. 1.
6. Carol Fleck and Sarah Kennedy, "Suspect Denied Bail after a Curse-Marked Hearing," *Philadelphia Inquirer*, October 31, 1985, p. 1.
7. Tom Torok, Laura Quinn, and Carol Fleck, "Suspect Is Described as Explosive Psychotic," *Philadelphia Inquirer*, October 31, 1985.
8. "Five Santa Cruz Slayings; Auto Only Clue," *Santa Cruz Sentinel*, October 20, 1970, p. 1.
9. Donald Lunde, *Murder and Madness* (San Francisco: San Francisco Book Company, 1976), p. 49.
10. "Just Who Is John Frazier?" *Santa Cruz Sentinel*, October 23, 1970, p. 2B.
11. Jay Shore, "Psychiatrist Claims Frazier Is Insane," *Santa Cruz Sentinel*, December 3, 1971, pp. 1, 7.

CHAPTER 5

1. Jonathan Kellerman, *Savage Spawn* (New York: Ballantine, 1999), p. 20.
2. William G. Kronenberger, http://medicine.indiana.edu, "Aggressive Youths, Violent Videogames Trigger Unusual Brain Activity," December 2, 2002.

CHAPTER 6

1. "Suspect's Mental State a Key Issue as Trial Starts Today in 13 Deaths," *New York Times*, June 6, 1983.

CHAPTER 7

1. Tom Lee, "Xerox Shooter Found Guilty," www.asianweek.com, June 15–21, 2000, p. 2.

CHAPTER 8

1. *Mass Murderers* (New York: Time-Life Books, 1992), p. 144.
2. Catherine Wessinger, *How the Millennium Comes Violently* (New York: Seven Bridges Press, 2000), p. 5.
3. "20th Century with Mike Wallace: Cults," A&E Network documentary, 2001.

CHAPTER 9

1. Catherine Wessinger, *How the Millennium Comes Violently* (New York: Seven Bridges Press, 2000), p. 135.
2. "Final Solution: Eichmann's Evidence on the Wannsee Conference," in Raul Hilberg, ed., *Documents of Destruction* (New York: Scholastic Library, 1971), pp. 99–106.
3. Fred E. Katz, *Ordinary People and Extraordinary Evil* (Albany: State University of New York Press, 1993), p. 5.
4. Ibid., p. 109.

CHAPTER 10

1. Ed Magnuson, "The Devil Made Him Do It," *Time*, April 9, 1990.

CHAPTER 11

1. Michael Kelleher, *Flash Point: The American Mass Murderer* (Westport, Conn.: Praeger, 1997), p. 154.
2. Gregg McCrary, *The Unknown Darkness: Profiling the Predators Among Us* (New York: Morrow, 2003), p. 226.

Bibliography

"All American Boy." *Newsweek,* August 15, 1966.

Altman, Jack, and Marvin Ziporyn. *Born to Raise Hell.* New York: Grove Press, 1967.

American Psychiatric Association. *Diagnostic and Statistical Manual of Mental Disorders.* 4th ed. Washington, D.C.: American Psychiatric Association, 1994.

America's Most Wanted. The John List case. 1986.

"Arizona Slayer of Five Convicted." *New York Times,* October 25, 1967.

Athens, Lonnie. *The Creation of Dangerous Violent Criminals.* Chicago: University of Illinois Press, 1997.

Attwood, Alan, and Philip Chubb. "Bloody Sunday." *Time,* August 18, 1987.

Aubrey, Jack. "Haunted by Lépine." *The Gazette,* December 2, 1990.

Berger, Meyer. "Veteran Kills 12 in Mad Rampage on Camden Street." *New York Times,* September 6, 1949.

"Besieged Slayer Talks with Reporter on Phone." *Philadelphia Inquirer,* September 6, 1949.

Blumenthal, Ralph. "87 Die in Blaze at Illegal Club." *New York Times,* March 26, 1990.

"Boy Escapes Unruh's Shots, Almost Suffocates in Closet." *Philadelphia Inquirer,* September 7, 1949.

"Brain Scans Show Pattern in Violent Behavior." www.cnn.com. July 27, 2000.

"Brain's Inability to Regulate Emotion Linked to Impulsive Violence." www.scienceagogo.com. July 30, 2000.

Breault, Marc, with Martin King. *Inside the Cult.* New York: Signet, 1993.

Brockman, Jason, and Erin McDanal. "The Alfred Packer Collection at the Colorado State Archives." Colorado State Archives.

Bugliosi, Vincent, and Curt Gentry. *Helter Skelter.* New York: W. W. Norton, 1974.

Capote, Truman. *In Cold Blood.* New York: Random House, 1966.

"Children Who Survived Massacre Say They Saw Man Kill Relatives." *New York Times,* June 8, 1983.

Churchill, Ward, and Jim Vander Wall. *Agents of Repression.* 2nd ed., Cambridge, Mass.: South End Press, 2001.

Cleckley, Hervey. *The Mask of Sanity.* St. Louis, Mo.: C. V. Mosby, 1941.

"Cult Members Say Solar Temple Leaders Ordered Mass Suicides." www.rickross.com. April 19, 2001.

Davis, Eric. "Solar Temple Pilots." *Village Voice,* October 25, 1994.

Di Marco, Roxy. "Slayer Missed His First Target." *Philadelphia Inquirer,* September 6, 1949.

Dietz, Park. "Mass, Serial, and Sensational Homicides." *Bulletin of the New York Academy of Medicine,* 62 (1986): 477–491.

Doucet, Clarence. "No Trace of Sniper Found after Police Comb Hotel." *Times-Picayune,* January 9, 1973.

Douglas, John. *Mindhunter.* New York: Scribner, 1995.

Douglas, John, Ann W. Burgess, Allen G. Burgess, and Robert K. Ressler. *Crime Classification Manual.* San Francisco: Jossey-Bass, 1992.

Eastham, Mike. *The Seventh Shadow.* Toronto: Warwick, 1999.

Eshleman, Russell, Mark Butler, and David Lee Presston. "Woman Opens Fire on Shoppers at Springfield Mall." *Philadelphia Inquirer,* October 31, 1985.

Everitt, David. *Human Monsters: An Illustrated Encyclopedia of the World's Most Vicious Murderers.* New York: Contemporary Books, 1993.

Ewing, Charles Patrick. *Fatal Families.* Thousand Oaks, Calif.: Sage, 1997.

———. *Kids Who Kill.* New York: Avon, 1990.

Federal Bureau of Investigation. "Report to the Deputy Attorney General on the Events at Waco, Texas." www.usdojgov.com. October 8, 1993.

Flaccus, Gillian. "Experts: Oregon Cases Fit Familicide Profile." Associated Press, January 7, 2003.

Flock, Jeff. "Chilling Details of the Houston Child Killings." www.cnn.com. June 22, 2001.

Galanter, Marc. *Cults: Faith, Healing, and Coercion.* New York: Oxford University Press, 1989.

Garbarino, J. *Lost Boys: Why Our Sons Turn Violent.* New York: Free Press, 1999.

Goodstein, Laurie, and William Glaberson. "The Well-Marked Roads to Homicidal Rage." *New York Times,* April 9, 2000.

Haight, James A. "And Now, the Solar Temple." *Free Inquiry,* Winter 1994–1995.

Hansen, Randall G. "School Violence: Assessment of Dangerousness in the Schools." *Forensic Examiner,* May–June 2000.

Hare, Robert. *Psychopathy: Theory and Research.* New York: Wiley, 1970.

———. *Without Conscience: The Disturbing World of the Psychopaths Among Us.* New York: Pocket Books, 1993. Guilford reissue, 1999.

Hassan-Gordon, Tariq. "Solar Temple Cult Influenced by Ancient Egypt." *Middle East Times,* issue 18, 2001.

Heide, K. *Young Killers: The Challenge of Juvenile Homicide.* New York: Sage, 1998.

Herndon, Peter. *A Terrible Thunder.* New York: Doubleday, 1978.

Hilberg, Raul, ed. *Documents of Destruction: Germany and Jewry, 1933–1945.* New York: Scholastic Library, 1971.

Hoffer, Eric. *The True Believer: Thoughts on the Nature of Mass Movements.* New York: HarperCollins, 1951. Reissue, 2002.

Hoge, R. D., and D. A. Andrews. *Assessing the Youthful Offender: Issues and Techniques*. New York: Plenum, 1996.

Holden, Wendy. "It Is Like a Bad Dream, I Wish I Had Stayed in Bed," *Daily Telegraph*, September 30, 1987.

Holmes, Ronald M., and Stephen T. Holmes. *Murder in America*. 2nd ed. Thousand Oaks, Calif.: Sage, 2001.

"'I Ran Out of Bullets, Went Home,' Killer Says." *Philadelphia Inquirer*, September 6, 1949.

"Indictment of Ohta Suspect Sought." *Green Sheet and Cabrillo Times*, October 29, 1970.

Janis, Irving L. *Groupthink*. 2nd ed. New York: Houghton Mifflin, 1986.

Karr-Morse, Robin, and Meredith S. Wiley. *Ghosts from the Nursery: Tracing the Roots of Violence*. New York: Atlantic Monthly Press, 1997.

Katz, Fred E. *Ordinary People and Extraordinary Evil*. Albany: State University of New York Press, 1993.

Kaufer, Steve, and Jurg Mattman. *Workplace Violence: An Employee's Guide*. Palm Springs, Calif.: Workplace Violence Research Institute, 2001.

Kelleher, Michael D. *Flash Point: The American Mass Murder*. Westport, Conn.: Praeger, 1997.

———. *When Good Kids Kill*. Westport, Conn.: Praeger, 1998.

Kellerman, Jonathan. *Savage Spawn: Reflections on Violent Children*. New York: Ballantine, 1999.

"The Killer at Thurston High." *Frontline*, PBS network documentary, 1999.

Kronenberger, William G. "Aggressive Youths, Violent Videogames Trigger Unusual Brain Activity." http://medicine.indiana.edu. December 2, 2002.

Kuempel, George. "Sniper's Terror Reign with 15 Dead, 34 Wounded." *Daily Texan*, August 2, 1966.

Lane, Brian. *Chronicle of Twentieth Century Murder*. Vol. 2. New York: Berkley, 1995.

Lane, Brian, and Wilfred Gregg. *The Encyclopedia of Mass Murder*. New York: Carroll and Graf, 2004.

Lassiter, D. *Killer Kids*. New York: Pinnacle, 1998.

Lavergne, Gary M. *A Sniper in the Tower: The True Story of the Texas Tower Massacre*. New York: Bantam, 1997.

Ledoux, Joseph. *The Emotional Brain*. New York: Simon & Schuster, 1996.

Lee, George F. "Seven Dead in Nimitz Highway Xerox Shooting." *Honolulu Star-Bulletin*, November 2, 1999.

Levin, Jack, and James Alan Fox. *Mass Murder: America's Growing Menace*. New York: Plenum, 1985.

Leyton, Elliott. *Sole Survivor: Children Who Murder Their Families*. New York: Pocket, 1990.

Lifton, Robert Jay. *The Nazi Doctors: Medical Killing and the Psychology of Genocide*. New York: Perseus, 1986.

Linedecker, Clifford. *Babyface Killers*. New York: St. Martin's Press, 1999.

———. *Killer Kids*. New York: St. Martin's Press, 1993.

———. *Massacre at Waco, Texas*. New York: St. Martin's Press, 1993.

"The Long Island Railroad Massacre." A&E Network documentary, 1996.

Lunde, Donald T. *Murder and Madness.* San Francisco: San Francisco Book Company, 1976.

"Mad Camden Killer Spirited to State Asylum at Trenton." *Philadelphia Inquirer,* September 8, 1949.

"Madman Traces His Murder Path." *Philadelphia Inquirer,* September 7, 1949.

Magnuson, Ed. "The Devil Made Him Do It." *Time,* April 9, 1990.

Malcolm, Andrew. "Kansas Hometown Baffled by Violent End to Life of Mark Essex." *New York Times,* January 11, 1973.

Marshall, Bryce, and Paul Williams. *Zero at the Bone.* New York: Pocket, 1991.

Mass Murderers. Alexandria, Va.: Time-Life Books, 1992.

McCrary, Gregg, with Katherine Ramsland. *The Unknown Darkness: Profiling the Predators Among Us.* New York: HarperCollins, 2003.

Meloy, J. Reid, ed. *The Psychology of Stalking.* San Diego, Calif.: Academic Press, 1998.

———. *Violent Attachments.* Northvale, N.J.: Jason Aronson, 1992.

Monahan, J., and H. J. Steadman. *Violence and Mental Disorder.* Chicago: University of Chicago Press, 1994.

Monahan, John, E. P. Mulvey, L. H. Roth, T. Grisso, and S. Banks. *Rethinking Risk Assessment: The MacArthur Study of Mental Disorder and Violence.* New York: Oxford University Press, 2001.

Moran, Sarah. *The Secret World of Cults.* Surrey, England: CLB International, 1999.

Murray, John. "TV Violence and Brainmapping in Children." *Psychiatric Times* 18, no. 10 (October 2001).

"Musician Denies Solar Temple Murders." *The Scotsman* (Edinburgh), April 18, 2001.

Nash, Jay Robert. *Bloodletters and Badmen.* New York: M. Evans, 1973. Revised ed., 1995.

Newton, Michael. *Waste Land.* New York: Pocket, 1998.

Niehoff, Debra. *The Biology of Violence.* New York: Free Press, 1999.

Noll, Richard. *The Encyclopedia of Schizophrenia and the Psychotic Disorders.* 2nd ed. New York: Facts on File, 2000.

O'Connor, Eileen. "Medical Expert: Brain Damage Could Have Contributed to School Shooting Spree." www.cnn.com. November 10, 1999.

Orion, Doreen. *I Know You Really Love Me: A Psychiatrist's Account of Stalking and Obsessive Love.* New York: Dell, 1998.

Palmer, Susan. "Purity and Danger in the Solar Temple." *Journal of Contemporary Religion,* October 1996.

Parker, Grant. *Mayday.* Perry, Mich.: Parker Press, 1980.

Pearson, Patricia. *When She Was Bad: How and Why Women Get Away with Murder.* New York: Penguin, 1997.

Raine, Adrian, et al. "Brain Abnormalities in Murderers Indicated by Positron Emission Topography." *Biological Psychiatry* 42, 1997.

———. "Interaction Between Birth Complications and Early Maternal Rejection in Predisposing Individuals to Adult Violence." *American Journal of Psychiatry,* September 1997.

Reang, Putsata. *Deadly Secrets.* New York: Avon, 2001.

Reinhardt, James M. *The Murderous Trail of Charles Starkweather.* Springfield, Ill.: Charles C. Thomas, 1960.

Ressler, Robert, and Tom Schactman. *Whoever Fights Monsters.* New York: St. Martin's Press, 1992.

Rieber, Robert W. *Psychopaths in Everyday Life.* New York: Psyche-Logo Press, 2004.

Roche, Timothy. "Andrea Yates: More to the Story." *Time,* March 16, 2002.

Ryzuk, Mary. *Thou Shalt Not Kill.* New York: Popular Library, 1990.

Sack, Kevin. "Gunman Slays 9 at Brokerage in Atlanta." *New York Times,* July 29, 1999.

Salamon, Julie. *Facing the Wind.* New York: Random House, 2001.

Samenow, Stanton. *Inside the Criminal Mind.* New York: Crown, 1984.

Santa Cruz County: A Century. Santa Cruz, Calif: Santa Cruz Sentinel Publishers, 1999.

Santa Cruz Sentinel. October 1970–December 1971.

Sapolsky, Robert. "Taming Stress." *Scientific American* 289, no. 3 (September 2003).

Scott, Gini Graham. *Homicide: One Hundred Years of Murder in America.* Los Angeles: Lowell House, 1998.

Scott, Margaret. *Port Arthur: A Story of Strength and Courage.* Melbourne, Australia: Random House, 1997.

Scott, Marian. "Campus Massacre." *The Gazette,* December 7, 1989.

Serrill, Michael S. "Remains of the Day." *Time,* October 24, 1994.

Sharkey, Joe. *Death Sentence: The Inside Story of the John List Murders.* New York: Signet, 1990.

Smith, Helen. *The Scarred Heart: Understanding and Identifying Kids Who Kill.* Knoxville, Tenn.: Callisto, 2000.

Smith, Wilfred. "Mad Camden Veteran Shoots Twelve Dead, Wounds Four in Mass Murder Orgy." *Philadelphia Inquirer,* September 6, 1949.

"Spanish Cops Arrest Cult Leader." Associated Press, January 8, 1998.

Spenser, Suzy. *Breaking Point.* New York: St. Martin's Press, 2002.

Starrs, James E. "Victims Exhumation Project." *Scientific Sleuthing Review* 13, no. 3 (summer 1989).

"Text of Psychiatrist's Notes on Sniper." *New York Times,* August 3, 1966.

Thorwald, Jürgen. *The Century of the Detective.* New York: Harcourt, Brace, and World, 1965.

Tomlinson, Gerald. *Murdered in Jersey.* New Brunswick, N.J.: Rutgers University Press, 1997.

Transcript of Andrea Yates's confession. *Houston Chronicle,* February 21, 2002.

"Unruh's Mother Faints When Told of Murders; Killer Guarded in Cell." *Philadelphia Inquirer,* September 9, 1949.

Wessinger, Catherine. *How the Millennium Comes Violently.* New York: Seven Bridges Press, 2000.

Whitcomb, Christopher. *Cold Zero: Inside the FBI Hostage Rescue Team.* New York: Little, Brown, 2001.

Yamanaka, Sharon. "Serial Murders in Santa Cruz County." www.santacruzpl.org/history/crime/8/12-2003.

Index

About the Author

KATHERINE RAMSLAND teaches forensic psychology at DeSales University in Pennsylvania and has published 23 books, including *The Science of Cold Cases*, *The Criminal Mind*, and *The Forensic Science of C.S.I.* She writes about forensic science, forensic investigation, and crime cases for Court TV's *Crime Library* and frequently contributes articles on forensic issues to *The Philadelphia Inquirer*. Dr. Ramsland has consulted on court cases, offered seminars on both writing and crime, and has been featured on numerous documentaries. She also co-wrote *The Unknown Darkness* with former FBI profiler Gregg McCrary.